A Blessed Journey

A Life Story of a Dreamer from Kenya
John Nganga Wamatu

PUBLICATION
CONSULTANTS
We Believe In The Power Of Authors

8370 Eleusis Drive, Anchorage, Alaska 99502-4630
books@publicationconsultants.com—www.publicationconsultants.com

ISBN Number: 978-1-63747-391-7
eBook ISBN Number: 978-1-63747-392-4

Library of Congress Number: 2024906706

Manufactured in the United States of America

CONTENTS

ACKNOWLEDGEMENTS

Glory and honor be to God. I wish to dedicate this memoir to our three boys, James Wamatu, Stephen Nganga, and Peter Karanja who have always believed in me and have been great companions. It is also in memory of our oldest son, James Wamatu Nganga, who encouraged me to write it and was kind enough to set up Grammarly for me. The fact that James loved writing and had some journalistic talent gave me hope and the feeling that our family had the potential to become authors. I thank my youth-time friends, Kung'u Kimani, Ngugi Keeru, George Mutembura, Gathenge Marima, Mugo Kagotho, and Mbaari Ngugi, for their outstanding comradeship in my life's journey. I thank my wife, Veronica Wanjiku Nganga, for always being there for me throughout the journey from the first time we met. I thank my family and friends for cheering me up along the way.

PREFACE

I always wanted to write something, a novel, a biography, or a set of essays, but something always held me back. Now is the time to sit and compose that magnificent manuscript. The urge to write up and finish my manuscript comes once in a while, but a time will come when it will be too late to write something. So, I have vowed to scribble something whenever the urge comes and when I get time to write. It does not happen that often, but my heart is willing, and my mind is ready to share something from inside me. In my primary school days, I had two very inspiring guys who were classmates of mine with similar dreams.

We thought we would become great and famous authors. People from all over the world would come to know and respect us. The main inspiration was the superb storytelling style in storybooks or novels we read then. The stories sounded so sweet and moving, and we kept reading more and more to enjoy the endless flow. We could not resist that temptation. One would go for hours bolted to that fountain of words that renewed the interest to get more and more. The sweet flow of words moved us, and we resolved to start writing with similar styles to make our readers enjoy our writing as much as we enjoyed books written by others.

We began writing manuscripts and would edit them ourselves for each other. The manuscripts were concise and only a few pages long. They were an attempt to become creative and tell excellent stories. We went on to write manuscripts, but we all became too busy in high school and stopped to write. We all attended different schools, and our communication became more and more difficult. Those were the days when the means of communication were poor. Somebody would send letters through the post office, but one could only receive mail at the local school or church. My would-be co-authors were all in different schools, making our communication difficult then. Eventually, we stopped communicating and finally did not write anymore, and we lost touch. I would write a little, stop, then start again in my learning. That determination to keep writing would come and go over the years.

When doing literature in English in high school, I renewed my zeal to write, but this, too, only went for a short time. Schoolwork during high school, university, and later work-related commitments stole the show, and writing got pushed back further and further. The fact that agriculture and plant breeding were my dearest subjects made my mind deal more with science than art. My first book-like publication was a dissertation I wrote as my Master of Science thesis in plant breeding.

The publication of my PhD thesis in 1999 was the next step. I further published a few papers in scientific journals, but these are different material forms. After retirement, I received a lot of encouragement from the family to at least get down and scribble. I would sit and start writing, get bored, and then not feel like writing for a while. I would have had a lot done, but Writer's block has always pulled me back repeatedly, leading to time wastage. If I manage to put something together, this is a great deal. I hope you enjoy reading this Memoir.

John Nganga Wamatu

Introduction

My life has been a journey of self-discovery. This memoir is an attempt to put together a few occurrences that made my life exciting and worth describing, even if by only a few words. I have found myself in perpetual competition with others for almost everything every step of the way. This competitive spirit is the driving force that kept me in check, made me compare myself with others, and changed one or two strategies to stay competitive and keep up. This feeling of having perceived competition with others has become a real motivation to work hard to be a winner, not a loser. This state of motivation was the common thread that knitted all aspects of my life. It started as early in my life as I can remember.

At a very young age, I would try to do things better or faster than my siblings. Once I finished the task, I felt fantastic when my siblings begged me to help them complete their allocated tasks. I would help them and feel great while sitting around very grateful people. This spirit of satisfaction would happen after many different tasks involving specified measurements. Our parents would also add to the satisfaction when they congratulated all of us for a job well done. Competition between my siblings and I was in every aspect of our lives, but we would combine it with cooperation in the end, making everyone feel happy afterward.

At primary school, competition between my classmates and I was evident as we tried to outdo each other whenever we felt like we did not measure up. When doing woodwork or arts and crafts lessons in middle and primary school grades, I would make the best statue or hat, trying to be the best. At high school and higher learning institutions, achieving better academic success was the primary source of motivation. This success would become a survival tactic when subjects became more burdensome, and only the best could remain. One would then select those subjects that they enjoyed most and those in which their performance was highest. The work-related competition involved many emotions and had remarkable attributes to it. Sometimes, it was your relationship with the boss that counted. In some cases, it was your competence that determined all. Most of the time, a combination of factors determines your success, making living even more enjoyable.

A person's life is a journey that largely depends on what the maker had in mind when he put his fingers to work. These fingers played their role, as the maker's brain planned. The maker knows about the details of the whole journey but will wait to give directions. The individual tries to decipher the hidden details of the maker's plan but can only make a slight scratch on them. He then puts this sketchy plan into action but can only go so far. This lack of progress is because the most critical details are unclear, and he goes forward as life flows. This lack of clarity leads to making vague choices, and one follows some doubtful paths that are sometimes right or sometimes wrong.

The individual is born into this world and fits into a body with genes that determine his joys and pains as he grows from a child to a grown-up. The individual grows up learning from the world and contributes his knowledge to make the world better than he found it. For this to work correctly, the community from which the individual comes directs his actions, producing results of that individual's performance. In this memoir, the reader will get a taste of different experiences in different stages of my life. Some of these experiences shaped my path in the muddy waters of life, shaping some of my performances and actions as fate would have it. Early childhood events led to instilling some characteristics that inhibit or encourage aspects of positive or harmful behavior. A case in point here is the occurrence that instills fear or respect in a young person, shaping other later events in life. This life journey was a great time when the young and energetic man trod the earth and enjoyed being in an overwhelming world where everything looked and felt strange but exciting.

When you come to, you discover yourself surrounded by people who show you total closeness and commitment.

Well, they are your people. One can never really forget to thank all humans, good and bad, that one encounters during his life-long journey and the good or bad experiences. All the same, these people contribute to something in your character, to build it or to destroy it. You do things with these people, sometimes lovingly and enjoying every part of it. Sometimes, you hate and disapprove of every part of their encounter. In addition to encountering people, you meet many challenges, especially regarding survival, but you hope to conquer the unexplored wide world. Sometimes, the places you visit give you a taste of good or bad experiences, making you choose or reject them.

It finally dawns on us, and we realize that so much is unknown and that much will remain hidden from our understanding. The little scratch we make must satisfy us because it equals our understanding and divine revelation. What remains hidden is for others to find out when the time comes. Life seems random, but my experience has shown me that everything follows a distinct pattern that varies from individual to individual. There must indeed be God who directs every movement in an adequately organized pattern of events, leading to each individual going through unique troubles and blessed moments. Such life-changing moments can only leave them without a word to explain how it all happened because they realize that theirs was only a role play in a drama of life directed by a superior power that one can only imagine. This understanding makes some people sit back and thank God for the many occurrences on their watch. Sometimes, life happens too fast, and you have no time to reflect correctly. Events also compound each other and leave one disillusioned.

Sometimes, life takes too long, and one may ask questions without getting any answers. Therefore, one must be grateful for all the good happenings and appreciative of all the not-so-sweet experiences. Going to school for an education played a significant role in my life by opening me to many possibilities and setting up a background for my family's stability, financial security, and survival. The motivation came from the need to eradicate poverty in my family, which had, in the earlier days, made us feel discouraged and unworthy of anything good in life. In my educational life, I strived to reach the top, which involved going higher and higher, from a Bachelor of Science degree to a Master of Science degree and then a doctorate.

The main reason for this was to try to make a difference in my family and to pull up the family and community, if possible, from the ground up. It was an attempt to provide a light for young folks in the village to see that one of their own could also make a difference in his life and the lives of others. As an individual, one can only do so much. If you are not politically inclined, you are not likely to spend your hard-earned resources on development activities that the government or community should provide for the community. You only see the need to have much done but will not do much.

After training or attending school and getting some knowledge, the knowledge is essential in obtaining a job to use what has been learned for work. Work was a significant tool to get the resources needed to provide my family and me with a comfortable living by affording personal and social amenities. Work gave me a feeling of accomplishment and meaning. As you serve, you also get respect from the community and some satisfaction. I was using the rewards from work to derive a meaningful social life and give the family the financial security they needed. The family benefitted too when I used my salary to pay for school and college fees for our kids and those kids of others in the family who needed assistance at the time we could afford to be of help. In this memoir, I will attempt to show the most significant jobs I performed as life went on.

I did jobs that came my way for various reasons. My first job was volunteering in a bakery in high school. It was a holiday job, giving me some memorable experiences in the first year; I could not help applying again the following year. I got another opportunity to work the next year and enjoyed it very much. This unique attachment is perhaps why I ended up loving to eat bread, and I still crave it. I did some of the jobs with the sole purpose of earning money for survival and trying to meet my needs. The truth was that the little money I received was chasing too many needs and was not enough for me to feel accomplished. This money was for survival rather than for meeting my needs. It was living from hand to mouth. In some other circumstances, like when I migrated to the United States and much later in life, the money I received could satisfy my needs, and work at this time had another meaning or purpose. At this time, work meant achieving the goals set by the employer. This meaning of work also differed from when I finally worked in retirement. The work I did then had the most significance for me because I did what I wanted to do whenever I wanted. I had or could get the money I needed for the necessities of life and could do whatever I wanted as long as I was not asking to buy a plane or own a cruise ship. My work was enough to meet my needs or as a routine work for earning money to care for the future.

Overall, I did my work with dedication and worked very hard, putting in all the necessary effort. I loved to work mainly because this was when I achieved the maximum returns. I would also work well with others when it came to solving issues in conjunction with others. The mighty hand of my creator worked miracles in every step I took, making the journey a blessed one.

John Nganga Wamatu

CHAPTER 1
Early Childhood Dreams

I started being aware of myself early in my life without fully comprehending what was going on, but continued fitting in as life happened. My vision kept widening as I moved on and became increasingly open to people and the environmental content every passing day. This opening up and appreciation took time, and it was a great joy just to get pulled in like the wind blows when it is calm and at a low speed but keeps going on and on. As a young person, I thought I was well protected and had many people around me to make me feel the warmth felt by plants in a greenhouse. I was filled with great thoughts for others around me and did not miss a thing.

I was doing something meaningful every day, receiving niceties from all and enjoying the overwhelming company of the people around me. My surroundings were pleasant, and everything was working as it should. Things could have been better, but we made no fuss about it. We kept wishing things would improve. At home and in our early ages, we lived in thatched houses with mud walls. We would go to the swamps with my mother and other ladies who would come to help her decorate the house. They would come with large baskets and sacks to get the clay soil, which is whitish swamp mud, to bring home to use on the outside part of the house walls covering the red volcanic mud on the inside.

In this way, the house would look like it has a white concrete finish. They would also bring that tall grass and use it for thatching. It was the ladies who did the thatching and wall decorations.

The community usually did the mud walls. Once a house was ready for applying the mud, my mother would cook some Githeri (mixture of boiled maize and beans) and some nice greenish Mukimo made with a few corn grains, Pigeon peas, pumpkin leaves, and potatoes pounded together. She would also cook some fermented porridge. Somebody would send out a word concerning the day of "ithinga," i.e., the day of applying mud. Many people from the community would come and mix soil and water in a large hole, enter the hole, and mix the mud with their feet. Some people would carry the mud in containers and deliver it to others, whose role was to apply the mud to the walls of the new house. Depending on their number, the people present completed the mud application to the walls. Sometimes, young people enjoyed playing local music and dancing to celebrate the new house.

Figure out a young boy with no shoes putting on an oversized coat and some khaki shorts that you do not see very well. That would be me or any of my brothers. Some impolite village girls from a better-off family would say they thought we were the market madman who used to wear similar clothes. Our father's used work uniforms were our special outfits, which always appeared oversized on us. We were always joyful and would run around our ten-acre farm every day, discovering a new place we had not been. It was a joyous time for us, mainly because we loved eating and tasting all the fruits on the farm, like oranges, mangoes, passion fruits, avocado, macadamia nuts, mbeera, etc., and products of the land, including cassava, sweet potatoes, and pineapples.

Our ancestral land was a piece of land that was rectangular. Only about four acres out of the whole farm had food crops. My father had supervised the planting of coffee on most of the farm, following directions of the Ministry of Agriculture, where he had worked as an agricultural assistant for many years. My father had several friendly colleagues from his place of work. Some of them came to visit him once in a while. We had to keep the compound always presentable. All children would be involved in pulling weeds growing along the way leading to the compound from the main road. We would manage all the bushes and grasses overgrowing along the way and prune the life hedge fence plants to size. Some plants along the hedge fence were Mukinduri (Croton megalocarpus) plants.

Somebody would train the fence plants to create a decent live fence. Other common plants that would make up the fence in some parts were Kei-apple (Dovyalis caffra Hook. f. & Harv.) Sim), and Kariaria (finger euphorbia or the pencil cactus), which is Euphorbia tirucalli in scientific terms. The finger euphorbia plant is commonly used in Kenya to mark property borders in those areas where it grows. The home compound clean-up exercise was routinely carried out during some national holidays like Christmas (December 25), Madaraka Day (June 1), and Jamhuri Day (December 12). On the farm, we grew corn, beans, pineapples, sweet potatoes, yams, and cassava, among other food crops. There were several Macadamia and mango trees on the farm.

We had two lemon trees and five orange trees. There were several papaya plants, too. These fruit trees remained productive for many years as we grew up, providing us with fresh fruits. There were banana plants scattered all over. All the food crops grew well due to the perfect growth conditions provided by the favorable weather patterns and the rich red volcanic soils in the region. We had two rain seasons that always provided enough water. These were the short rains (October-December) and the long rains (April-June). The main road from Gatundu town was west of our farm. To the east side, acting as the eastern borderline, flowed the water of the stream, Kiabira. The stream flowed from the north to the south. The farm was on a sloppy ridge sloping towards the stream.

Along the area up to fifty feet off the stream, coco yams (Colocasia esculenta) and sugarcanes would grow very well. We always had a large fenced rectangular field of about an acre on the farm, close to the main house. The fence would enclose the grass area and have three or four cows. Our compound had a three-bedroom main house, a kitchen, and a sheep and goats' stall. My father occupied one of the main house bedrooms while my mother occupied the other. The girls occupied the additional bedroom, and the boys stayed in the second room in the kitchen house. The cows grazed on the grass and would have enough feed by themselves except for the occasional corn stover thrown inside their paddock. Somebody would milk the cows every morning and evening. During the milking, we offered the cows some special feed from the feed store rich in proteins and other nutrients. I would occasionally be required to help with the milking of cows. Someone always had to go to the bushes to get plant branches as feed for sheep and goats. They would hang the goat feed inside their stalls. I would occasionally be tasked with this work sometimes.

In those early days of my youth, the road from Gatundu town to my home in Ituiku village was more like a path with a sharp, sloppy hill preventing cars from using it because they never made it up the ridge. The vehicles would go around the long route up to a mile towards the north and turn around at Gitati-ini to come down to my home. During the rainy seasons, vehicles would get stuck on this route in several places, where drainage could have been better and reaching home was only sometimes guaranteed. No wonder I always remember those days, meeting my neighboring grandfather daily, tending his large flock of sheep on the road for an extended part of the way. No cars passed through, and only one lorry driven by a neighbor named Kamunyo and owned by a coffee estate would go down the hill when coming to pick up coffee pickers. This lorry would be parked at our compound half a mile from his home due to poor road conditions and security reasons. This lorry was the focus of our excitement as children because it was the first we ever saw. We would admire it and touch it in every possible part. It was something to wonder about because most of us children never rode in a car until we turned teenagers. We wore no decent clothes until our teenage years.

I got used to eating a lot, which eventually became a problem. I formed the habit of eating anything I found people eating and going from one fruit tree to another to harvest and eat the ripe or unripe fruits. I would eat oranges, mangoes, avocadoes, sweet potatoes, and any tropical fruit or vegetable I came across during the day, ending most days with discomfort, stomach pain, and strange gases of undigested fiber from unripe or uncooked food. As kids around ten, we (the last boys in the family) would try to be innovative and creative in making toys to play with and find ways to entertain ourselves. We enjoyed several childhood games with toys made with locally available materials. One such game was the spinning of cones (kuhura mbira), where you would spin a cone and assess how long you could keep it spinning compared to another person. Another one was running while operating or moving a wheel like the rim of a bicycle or car tire, either with bare hands or a stake. We also enjoyed playing a chess-like game with bottle tops.

We would enjoy the toys that we would build ourselves. One idea involved making a two-wheel toy by cutting a tree disc and eating out the wood shavings in the middle, leaving an axle-like piece. One would connect a thin piece of six-foot-long wood with a wedge on one side to the disc.

One would place the side of the wood with no wedge on the shoulder, and the wedge part would loosely fit onto the two wheels in the middle of the axle. The driver would only drive the toy on flat surfaces. We called the toy "ngari ya kihonge," a wedge vehicle. I was particularly good at making this kind of play-thing that I had to leave a forever memorable mark on my left-hand thumb. I was making a new design of my favorite toy when I split off a quarter of the left side of the thumb using a machete, the tool of choice for this model. The other wooden cart-like vehicle, "ngari ya ikurura," or sliding vehicle, would be made by cutting four wooden discs or wheels from a tree of a suitable girth. One would join these wheels to the axles of a rectangular frame.

Somebody would connect a piece of wood to the front wheels to steer the cart. The back part of the sole would be used as the braking system but would be coordinated with the steering to reduce the speed effectively. It was advisable not to overspeed as this would sometimes lead to a lack of control. There were many times when we got injuries due to moving too fast downhill, and we would roll over many times depending on how steep the hill was. We would usually use a suitable tree, "Mubariti" -Grevillea Robusta, to cut out relevant pieces of wood for this work. This tree was grown for firewood, timber, and shade in the coffee fields. We had a shortfall of tools for this work and sometimes ended up tying pieces of wood together instead of using screws or nails. We would use a hand saw or a machete to cut off a thick piece of wood, which would take some time. We would make several such carts and use them to compete against one another by racing down the hills. Manufacturing toys and running with them was fun, and weekends were the best time to enjoy.

In some cases, there would be accidents, and someone would be badly injured, but this never stopped us from competing. If any of us boys found a toy of interest anywhere, we would collect it and bring it home for others to enjoy, however broken it might have been. Any new toy found was a real treasure. Sometimes, we would make used toy collections from dump sites of rich neighbors or manure piles delivered for farming purposes by lorries (very productive sometimes).

We were a family of nine children, with my father and mother raising three girls and six boys. We came from a humble background, and life was usually not taken for granted. We lived in a village where we practiced peasant farming and would grow food crops (corn, beans, Potatoes, etc., for our nourishment) and some cash crops like coffee, avocadoes, macadamia nuts, etc., for sale to obtain cash. The food crops would be grown from the main road to the area around the home compound. The food crops would usually last us up to the next harvest season, and therefore, this was equivalent to living from hand to mouth in a cycle that never changed.

Coffee as a cash crop was the primary source of money for the family and was grown in the area following food crops up to the lower but steep area of our sloping land. After coffee, it would be thickets with giant trees, bushes, and creeping plants, which stayed unused at the time due to the steepness of the land and entanglement from creeping diverse tropical plants. In these thickets, we occasionally harvested wild fruits like passion fruits that grew wildly and in large numbers. There were also many raspberries and blackberries to enjoy if you could make a path or a way through the thickets.

Proceeds from coffee sales were unreliable, untimely, and insufficient to satisfy all the demands. One expected that the coffee proceeds would be enough to pay off all the debts incurred to produce it. Other debts, including home running expenses and payment of children's school fees, were to be cleared by the coffee proceeds. My mother managed the food crops budget while my father was responsible for the cash crops. The main labor-intensive tasks were weeding for the coffee plants, harvesting coffee berries, pruning, and herbicide spraying. My siblings and I were the primary source of family labor for the coffee field weeding, but we could occasionally get some ladies who came to do some of the weeding for food crops and coffee picking. The coffee field comprised one block with a footpath running in the middle. We used this path to connect the home compound and the stream. The path was very important for fetching water from the stream. Some benches were well-formed along the route and acted as resting areas along this path. The resting places would have shade from the scattered Grevillea Robusta trees in the coffee field. One would rest at about ten or so places along the route. The coffee spacing distance was nine feet in benches.

Every time, we would get a task to weed from the footpath to one end per day per person. I would wake up early, do my allocated task, sit down, wait for others to come, and beg for help. I would feel thrilled and highly fulfilled. Coffee production demands high-quality standards, achieved through the labor-intensive selective harvesting system. In my area, we picked coffee every Tuesday and Saturday. When harvesting a coffee bush, we had different styles. We would be attracted to those trees with many red cherries that are easily bendable without breaking.

Once we select a tree, we would bend the tree, fit the top part of the bush between our legs, and selectively pull the berries from the branches out quickly. This way, you would be guaranteed to harvest a lot. We were only paid for harvesting coffee if there was plenty to pick. Payments for coffee harvested motivated us a great deal. My oldest sister is known to have been the best at gathering the most coffee berries (1 to 2 big bags) and must have made the most from coffee harvesting. She was also the fastest among our siblings in pulling weeds for coffee. At the end of harvesting, my father would call everyone and tell them coffee harvesting was over and all harvesters should be at home. At this point, everyone would gather their harvest and bring it home in the designated sorting area with a tarp ready for the next step. Everyone would pour their harvest into the standard unit container and then run the coffee on the tarp for sorting. If this were a harvest with lots of coffee, my father would have money to pay everyone immediately.

Sorting on the tarp would follow with everyone working on the coffee berries. One would put aside different categories of berries, including overripe, unripe, green, and black dry cherries. Somebody would then gather and transport the various categories of berries separately. The lovely ripe red and unripe cherries would be delivered to the coffee factory on the same day as the grade one and grade two coffee produce categories. The green and dry black cherries would be combined and dried at the farm until they are evenly dried and delivered to the factory later.

I always loved to accompany the coffee produce during its delivery to the factory. Pick-up trucks would deliver the produce in bags to the factory. We would ride the truck on top of the coffee bags. Once the coffee was in the factory, one would have to form queues waiting for the coffee to be weighed and recorded by the factory clerks. In a coffee cherry, the fruit encases the seeds or beans. At the factory, processing starts with pulping. In the pulping process, the outer skin is separated from the beans. The method used is the wet process method, where water separates the pulp from the beans using screens in a well-thought-out process.

In the rare events where we would make some money from coffee cherry picking, we would use the funds to run our small enterprises, like keeping chickens, which would lay some eggs that we could sell to make some money. Each person would also run a small garden and grow crops of one's choice to sell them at harvest for a profit. Most of us were enterprising, although some were always better. I was usually somewhere in the middle. My oldest sister was always the best in this regard and was the admiration of all. She would closely be followed by my eighth-born brother, who appeared to succeed in anything he put his fingers on.

It was never clear how my father managed the coffee proceeds, but we dared not ask where the money was or how much it was. Mother also dared not ask about it. I learned that most homes were like that or even worse. There were stories of how some men would occasionally lose all their coffee or tea proceeds to women doing business in the city. We knew we could positively tell when my father had received some money. That day, my father would buy three to four kilograms of meat(beef), and he would personally chop up the meat for stew and separate it from the individual pieces for roasting by all the family members.

Each person in that compound would get a specific piece of meat dedicated to them by my father, and they would personally roast the particular piece of meat on the grill and eat it. It would be a great day because everyone loved meat, and there was nothing as good as knowing that the food you enjoyed that evening would have meat as an ingredient, a very rare one. On such a meat day, I always prayed to be around so that my father would select me to help him chop the meat. If chosen for such an honor, you got a massive piece of meat, and you would be the man to go to if someone wanted to know which piece of meat was theirs. The particular meat treat was repeated on major national holidays, at which time my father would give us this treat and even make his special dish called 'Rothi,' which was a very delicious food with fried meat chunks served with fried whole potatoes. No one in the family learned how to make this dish. Our father obtained all the groceries through credit and paid the shopkeeper when he got his salary at the end of the month.

My father would write a note to the shopkeeper named Kung'u, Son of Gikurumi, and send us to the shopkeeper to collect what he wrote down on the note to the shopkeeper. My father had a unique cursive handwriting that we could not imitate. The shopkeeper knew my father's handwriting and signature, and we could never alter anything despite always having this temptation. My father would order for six pounds of maize flour, a full bar of soap, 2 KG of cooking fat, 2 KG of sugar, and 2 KG of beans. He would sign the note and state that he was James Wamatu, son of Nginduri. The shopkeeper always carefully followed my father's instructions, and we would go home carrying baskets full of food. We were grateful to God to have had a father who could provide for our needs. We always compared ourselves to other neighbors and found ourselves quite privileged. Of course, some families had almost nothing, and others seemed to have everything.

Some days were better than others. Sleeping conditions were not very hygienic, and we shared beds. There were only two beds for eight kids. The two beds had some bedding but were only sometimes that clean due to dirty boys like me not washing my feet properly at night (this was the requirement). The unclean beddings invited visitors every night in the form of lice, fleas, and bed bugs. Jiggers would infest the feet, making life somewhat complicated if you put your mind to it. The best policy was to live without being pulled down by such distractions. This was possible, and most people managed not to show any sign of weakness and always put up a brave face but had untold suffering within them. This did not, however, steal our joy, and we always appreciated our way of life with a stride.

CHAPTER 2

My Immediate Family

I had my parents, brothers, and sisters to thank for my great experiences growing up. My father was a real gentleman and a man loved in society. He had one brother and four sisters. He had inherited ten acres of land from his father, a well-known shepherd with hundreds of sheep and goats. The family had lost a lot of land previously owned by my grandfather during land boundary division in colonial times when my father and others went to detention camps due to their stand concerning the independence of Kenya. When I came to know my father, I realized that he was dedicated to his family and was working very hard to ensure his children had enough to eat and to go to school.

These were the most essential qualities of a father at the time due to the lack of adequate resources and little growth in the development of our country. Most parents in my community had not set their goals to allow them to succeed in these two qualities and just lived their lives like rolling stones that gathered no moss. They ended up not being responsible for their children and not completing their education. The community was paternalistic, with fathers being the community's leaders and heads of homesteads. My father had some education that allowed him to read and write and get a job as an agricultural assistant.

My father taught me many things, including humility, kindness, gratitude, patience, love, gentleness, hard work, and many other virtues that space here may not suffice to describe all. An example of humility was when he told us to tread cautiously, even if we were the proud owners of a shop and a grain mill. At the time, successful individuals in the area owned these two businesses.

One famous farmer had a coffee estate, a grain mill, and a big chunk of land left for him by a white settler who left after independence. Whenever we shared a drink with my father, he would become highly grateful and show happiness and gladness to the extent of singing songs he would randomly put together. The best of those were: Nuu warakaria Muru wa Nginduri...? Hello...hello...hello ndakanarakare" Translated this means: "Who angered the son of Nginduri....? Hello...hello...hello he should never be angered". Another was: "Kaba ndukiriruo rurie rwa Bathi.... Ndigatukiriruo kwa Ndumbi. Ndumbi Mburu.... Mburu niarekwo ataware...." This means: "I would rather be late in Bathi's valley....and never be late in Ndumbe's valley. Ndumbe the son of Mburu.... Mburu is to be allowed to rule the valley…" Yet another one of his sayings…. "Urogitwo ni nyukwa," which we never understood. My father's encouragement helped me excel in school and become a tough cookie. I thank my father for providing me with school uniforms from primary school to high school.

Additionally, my father paid all my school fees, making me forever grateful. He also raised the school fees for my nine siblings, paying fees for each one to the level they could manage. This fact made my father glad, judging from his reaction, when I thanked him for ensuring I was never sent home by the school for not paying my fees. He was so glad about this; he could not help telling my siblings how happy he got when I showed him my gratitude.

Despite not having had much formal education, my mother was a great lady and teacher. She had been brought up near where our local town later developed and about two miles from where my father grew up. She had three brothers and two sisters. She was the last-born child of my grandparents, and all her siblings lived within a radius of six miles from each other. When my mother was young, her parents requested her to become their Shepherd, so that her youngest brother, Kariuki, could attend school and represent the family. Her parents believed that a woman could never become an office clerk.

Unfortunately, this was open discrimination against women. Discrimination against women was common among our Agikuyu tribe. The men did not welcome any challenge from women. Many girls missed out on school.

Her brother Kariuki was my favorite uncle and went to school to become a Physician Assistant in our town; he passed as a town doctor and was our family doctor. He was the first person to own and drive a Dodge car in our city and the area where cars were countable on one hand.. We would all be taken to him for treatment whenever we got sick. This uncle later became very important to me because he closely predicted my future. Long before he knew much about me, he said I would eradicate rats from his sister's homestead. The prediction of my success in life proved my uncle was right! My mother taught me multiple lessons on patience, love, kindness, goodness, faithfulness, gentleness, and self-control.

My family and I have enjoyed and continue to experience great graces from the almighty God in our lives, and we believe these excellent tidings stem from my mother's prayers and blessings. She taught me to recognize the importance of everyone around me because there are times when hard times hit, and the only available help may come only from those near me. There were so many occasions when we had difficult financial times, and my mother would get out and find food from well-to-do relatives or work with my sisters wherever there was work to earn us a living. She would become active, especially during drought, and ensure we did not starve. There were many occasions when she would send my sisters to an uncle or an aunt to get food. Sometimes, it would be a bunch of bananas, a sack of corn grains, beans, or even cassava or sweet potatoes. We knew we would have enough to eat every time they returned from such trips. Without the borrowed food, it would be a stormy night when we would sleep hungry. On such nights, my mother would place some inedible male coco yams in a boiling pot where they would stay the whole night without getting cooked. The kids would wait for them to cook, fall asleep, and go to bed.

My mother would throw away the uncooked yams once the kids fell asleep. I vividly remember some days my mother would take my sisters to harvest coffee in the coffee estates around the famous Kenyatta Road. The Coffee plantations would send their lorries to our town and community villages where we lived, and coffee pickers would get into these trucks and go to work. My mother and my sisters would be such customers. They would get up early in the morning and be transported to the plantations to pick coffee. They would receive a wage that depended on how many 20 kg containers of coffee berries they harvested at the end of the day. The money would take care of our food for a couple of days, and then they would go to the plantations again if my father had not brought more resources. We, five boys, would be left at home to do some chores, including weeding for coffee trees and fetching water and firewood.

Of course, we would surely mess around and sometimes even try to cook whatever we could with any leftover food to fill our stomachs. The stomach seemed to be the most significant motivation for our actions. We would even look for corn cobs from the leftover stover, roast those cobs, and eat the few available grains. I am grateful to my mother for having bought me my first pair of shoes and casual clothes, not forgetting my Sunday best clothes from early childhood through my teenage years. She would ensure that her kids had decent clothes to go out of the home with, especially on Sundays. My mother taught me to love others without remembering their faults. Her love for my family and me was unmistakable.

My mother showed us her love by cooking food for our children, feeding them, and caring for them the whole day for no payment when my wife and I were at work. My siblings would become envious and complain that my mother did not love them as much as she loved me and my family. Through her, I learned to reconcile different parties within the family and between the family members and the parents. Seeing the two warring parties communicating again after I pleaded with them to seek reconciliation was a joy. My mother always gave us some examples of patient people who succeeded in life due to being patient.

She was herself a great example! She told us that at the very beginning, when our eldest brother was about six years old, they were having great difficulties with food during a drought at home, and my father had decided to bring in a second wife. The new wife could not tolerate the home problems and decided to move away. My mother tried to plead with her to stay so they could share the issues, but she went away anyway. My mother was patient enough to wait through the hard times to tell the stories. She always advocated for kindness to strangers and was an understanding mother-in-law who accepted new daughters-in-law with kindness and goodness.

When completely new to our home, my wife became accepted as my wife through the graces of God and the incredible warmth of my parents, brothers, and sisters. This warmth was so good that some of my siblings thought my parents loved me more than they were. We only treated my parents with respect, and they showed us immense love in return. It became worse when my mother took care of our kids, making some of my siblings say that we had made our mother a maid for our children. The truth is that she loved those kids very much!

This great warmth helped my wife and I cement our togetherness, and we cannot thank all those involved enough. When we were very young, we learned to be grateful to our mother whenever she gave us something, regardless of what it may have been. We would tell her a prayer that would come out automatically: "Thengiu Mami, urorathimwo ni Ngai uture matuku maingi guku thi, "meaning "Thank you, Mom, may God bless you and give you many years on this earth," and indeed God took her at 92 years which was a great blessing considering that my father went to see the Lord at 77 years of age. My wife and I felt very honored when we were able to take outstanding care of my mother the whole time after my father died. The great care we gave our mother in her last days makes us believe it is our source of great blessings.

My oldest brother was way ahead of us in age to engage in our childhood experiences for the most part. He was friendly and outgoing and loved by people wherever he went. By the time I was ten, he was already thirty years old and had already worked for different companies as a storekeeper. He was very hard-working and trustworthy. He worked for the then-big construction companies, including Water Development, HZ, H-Young, Putt Sarajevo, etc., doing great projects including roads, water development, dams, etc. He loved his profession and was also very good at it, and the company managers wanted to keep him as long as he wished. In every company he worked for, he was very popular with his co-workers and would bring some of his friends home.

He would go to work for a month, then come home at the end of every month, bringing goodies for all his siblings. We would all hang around the home waiting for him to arrive with goodies. The older folks would be clever enough to go and be the first to meet him in our hometown. Those would get even better goodies from my brother. We all loved him because of the goodies and because he showed us genuine love. We never got disappointed. We would give him funny names like "Zeah," probably because his friends nicknamed him "Zala." My brother was most possibly nicknamed by his workmates "Zala" to make him have an Israelite name because they were working with an Israelite company with one Israelite named "Zevi." We would all get something from him, and my mother and sisters would cook great foods with meat as an ingredient.

Those days, meat was a delightful ingredient in any meal if one could afford it. With my sisters' help, my mother would make Chapati, and the whole place would smell great. This monthly occurrence would be a great deal for all the folks in the family who would look forward to it the following month, thereby keeping hope alive. Sometimes, when my brother came home, our cousin Gichini, a few years younger than our oldest brother, would visit and take some family pictures. He would also play some excellent music, which we had always looked forward to. Gichini was also a man of humor who was very funny and creative and would entertain us for hours. One joke he always told was that of a local old man who could not speak English but could read the name of a textbook, "Gateway to Form One," in the Agikuyu language as "Gatewai to Form One." This joke would make us laugh heartily! The same older man was also in another joke when he told his wife when she gave him food with a plate that their son had won in a marathon race. He was supposed to have said, "Kai kai Wani...i.ini ukunjikirira Irio gathani-ini karia kara ho... oo...tiruo ni Wakahiu, meaning "My wife Wanini, why do you give me food in that small plate won by our son Wakahiu?. Gichini used to call me a "Kimubirithi," meaning a "Policeman" due to my height.

He also used to joke about my reddish eyes, described by a man from Meru who was not fluent in the Agikuyu language, as being like those of a leopard. He would say in broken Kikuyu, "Maitho ma Nganga ri, no ta ma Cui," meaning, "Ng'ang'a's eyes are like those of a Leopard's." Gichini was also a renowned radio and watch repairer at the time. He had a very sharp mind when it came to radios, umbrellas, and watches. We needed something to make us feel hopeful. God bless my elder brother's soul for that nice briefcase he bought me when I passed my primary school examination and was joining high school. My briefcase gift greatly encouraged me to work hard and succeed in high school. I kept this briefcase for a long time, which is still in my storage room many years later.

He would also make all the Wamatu children glad at the end of every month when he would come from work and give everyone gifts according to their request. One of my sisters remembers him for taking her to high school on the first day. He is well known for what our mother always remembered him promising mother when he was young that he would be coming home at the end of every month after working for 30 days with such a heavy basket full of goodies, such that his body would be bending from the one side that had the hand carrying the basket.

My three sisters were also slightly removed from us in the kids' circle because they were already responsible people who could only send us here and there to ensure we were out of trouble. Each of the sisters had a particular role in our upbringing, and we had special respect for each other without prejudice because we truly loved them, and one can only say good things about our interactions with them. Our oldest sister was the second born in the family. She was very hard-working and knowledgeable. She would go with my mother to work at the coffee estates to earn some money for our much-needed additional funds. She was very responsible and would be sent on errands to look for food for the family.

The younger people in the family looked to her for guidance and counsel. She went to a school in Kahugu-ini, Kahugu-ini Secondary School, away from home. The sister in the middle of our three was the third born. She attended a secondary school in Murang'a district and became a primary school teacher. She was in charge of our entertainment and enlightenment. She was a very loving individual with a kind heart, very gentle and full of joy and love. She truly loved us, children, and she had a way of showing it through her great smile and many good deeds to us. Whenever she came home to visit, she always had some goodies for us kids, making us love her even more. She taught in faraway schools and would only come home after a long time. We would miss her a great deal, and we would be looking forward to our next eventful outing. She was always thinking of ways to enlighten us by organizing trips to the nearby town of Thika, allowing us to eat out in restaurants, and traveling out using her own money. We came to know about restaurants and other cities courtesy of her goodness. The youngest sister was the fourth born in the family. She was a very hard-working person who was proud of the family. She was kind-hearted and outgoing. She went to secondary schools in Murang'a and attended different schools where she did well.

Later, she went on to do the nursing course and become a nurse. She used this course to better the lives of all in the family. She is the one who renewed our parents' house and brought them development. She loved all the folks in the family and was very good at making alliances with different family members to bring some development. All boys remember her except the oldest for caring for us by carrying us on her back when we were children. For that, we will ever be grateful. The story goes that she once dropped brother number four, making him develop some permanent marks from burns on his behind. She was severely punished for it by our mother. I had a special relationship with this sister, and I remember visiting her in Murang'a once after sitting for my high school examination. The following day after arrival, I left her apartment where she lived and went to the town to do some sightseeing.

When my sister came home, a non-respectful neighbor described how I washed my only "rubber shoes" and waited until they were dry. I then put them on and went towards the town. When I returned, I was very unhappy with the neighbor's description of my poor man's shoes. This sister was like our family doctor, helping us all with our medical issues. If anything related to medical emergencies in the family arose, this sister would do everything possible to get a solution, regardless of whom it concerned. She was extremely helpful to our parents. My two immediate older brothers were born after my youngest sister, while my last two brothers came after me. These last four brothers were instrumental in shaping and modifying my life path. Our togetherness was mainly due to the comradeship and the rivalries we had to undergo. We were very close to one another, but we were competing for everything, including attention, love, food, shelter, and material things. Each one tried to shine brighter than the others. We would pretend we were great business people who owned many businesses and pretend that all customers were flocking to acquire their goods from one shopkeeper and not the other. Brother number three would always outshine the others if Brother number five did not already win since he was more progressive.

The others, including myself, were in between and could not compete. I remember the race for survival where the medium of exchange used for business was corn grains from roasted maize cobs, which would be food for the seller who sold certain inedible goods. We all took part in many fights among us five boys; sometimes, they did not end well. A case in point was that one time, brother number two became so angry that he threw a machete at me, cutting my left calf very severely. I lost a lot of blood, and he had to carry me to the hospital, following the back streets to have my leg stitched up with about twelve stitches, leaving a scar that is visible to date. Brother number two had a short fuse, got angry quickly, and was very good at throwing things at people. At one time, he threw a hammer in my direction and missed my head by a whisker!

The good Lord was always on our side during our challenging engagements. At other times, he would be pretty friendly and helpful. He would express love for others if he wanted to. I remember his generosity towards me when he visited me at school when he had just gotten a job. I shared some great moments with him. This brother also went to high school at Kahugu-ini Secondary School. Later, he worked with me at the Coffee Research Foundation. He did a lot at the research center to support his family. He worked there for over twenty years.

Brother number three was a real gentleman who always behaved well and it was nice being around him. As a child, he learned to be spontaneous and frank. He would tell facts about issues and things and call them as they were. We remember him refusing to eat food because it had cassava. He would refuse to eat and say, "Nie he Rwanga," meaning, "My, the food has Cassava!" and would cry, making the sound "nii...ii...iii..." and not eat the food just because it had some Cassava in it although this was the only available food. We often called him Kinii...ii...iii...", because of crying "nii...ii...iii..." He was wise and the man to go to if you wanted something tangible to be accomplished. He was effective in following up with processes. From far back to the present, I went through him for many issues I wanted to get done.

He had such a charm that made him very popular with all the siblings. His skin color was the lightest among all boys. He was polite and resourceful, and one learned to trust him for his charisma. This brother also attended Kahugu-ini Secondary School. My father loved him very much, most likely because he had named him after his brother. He would, however, be a little selfish, depending on the conditions. Brother number five was easy-going, humble, and very hard-working. He was always lucky and prosperous in matters that he tried. He was an elegant person but relatively quiet and introverted. Like most of my other siblings, this brother also attended Kahugu-ini Secondary School. He would be quite stingy sometimes and a little selfish. He usually competed with me and would bully the last-born brother greatly. The rivalry between the last two brothers and myself was the most intense. This brother later became very successful in business and had a thriving shop at Gatundu market at my father's premises. He led others to establish a shop that did very well for a few years.

This shop was an outstanding achievement, and it came to support many programs at home. The shop was also my source of funds whenever life became difficult in my earlier years under employment. I would borrow money from this shop now and then. I would pay up my debts mostly in time when I got my salary, except for one loan. This loan had something to do with me becoming a co-owner of a pickup truck (KJY 229) that we bought together with all the shop directors, including our youngest sister, brother number three, brother number five, and brother number six. I could not repay the loan until I relinquished my co-ownership rights. I had to do this because the shop directors continuously sent my father to me telling me to pay up. As you can imagine, this ruffled my feathers a great deal. Sometimes, I would get angry at my father and I lose my temper.

Brother number six was the last born. He had a pleasant personality and it was nice being around him. He was friendly as well as empathetic. He was quite imaginative and a good teammate. We both attended Ituru High School, and he learned a lot from me. He had been admitted to the school because he qualified to join it and due to my good reputation. I protected him from hazing, a big problem at the school. I used to compete with him for bread at home. Both of us loved bread. My mother knew this and would always make sure there was bread for her sons. We would be greedy and snatch almost a whole loaf of bread, squeeze it with our fingers, and eat without thinking of anyone else. Unfortunately, I wanted him to do well and pushed him too hard. My over-persuasion had negative results, especially when my parents had to compel me to let him be. In one notable incident, my parents denied me the right to borrow an advanced dictionary from him because he did not want me to have it. I had thought it was just what I needed at the time. Eventually, I had to leave school for advanced studies away from home. This move did not positively affect my brother's later performance at the school. After school, he worked at the shop with others for a few years. Shop businesses would later go down in the town as large wholesalers came to town and took over most of the business. Ordinary shops stopped doing well as the large wholesalers sucked them up and took away most of the business.

In our younger days, whenever my mother shared food, we would sit around our mother because she never used to eat all her food. She would eat a little and then give her remaining food to the child that was seated nearest to her. I would get it sometimes, or my brothers would, depending on God's grace or the stars' alignment. One had to be lucky. You would always sit on our mother's left- or right-hand side and try to be as close to her as possible. Eventually, the lucky kid would win the prize. The good thing was that if you were kind to the receiver, he could get you some of the food if he was in a good mood. We would also get a chance to be the first person to ask for the ugali pot to get those hard ugali leftovers that are so delicious! You only needed to shout, "Thaburia ngure!" meaning "Will take care of the Ugali pot!". This way, you get the whole pot and can share the leftovers with any interested person, but you become in charge. These leftovers were so delicious that even the older kids would scramble for them. We would fight for food and were greedy children who were hard to satisfy. I used to eat any food I got and would eat at any time I found something to eat. Lack of discipline in eating food was disastrous because the stomach would expand, have excess hydrochloric acid released in the stomach, and back up into the esophagus, causing heartburn and gas, making the person quite uncomfortable.

The process would happen daily, and I never used to learn from my evening troubles. I would find myself eating raw sweet potatoes, ripe bananas, mangoes, oranges, Githeri, Ugali, greens, and whatever got cooked. The lack of discipline was a dangerous way of life because it would make my tummy so full at the end of the day that I had to stay in that uncomfortable situation and fall asleep anywhere. I have a scar on my left leg just below the knee, which I got from a barbed wire fence. At around nine at night, we went to take water to the cows. My mother has just boiled Githeri and separated it from the water.

This water was said to have nutrients good for the cows. Since we had to wait for the cows to drink and take the containers back to the house, I decided to nap near the cow pen. The others, including sister number three, returned to the house when the cows finished drinking the water. At around eleven, my family was preparing to go to bed when they realized I was missing. They came out of the house calling my name, and my sister shouted, "Nganga, iyo Hiti!" which means "Nganga, there comes a Hyena!" I quickly woke up and ran away without knowing that I was inside a place fenced with barbed wire. The barbed wire got me good, leaving a big and very long wound with a lot of blood loss.

CHAPTER 3

Primary School Notables

In our day, you would enter class one of primary school only when you can touch the ear on the opposite side of the head. I was able to do this in 1969 when I was eight years old. I was one year older than some kids, although we also had other older kids. We had to walk northwest from home for about one and a half miles to reach Ichaciri Primary School. A boy scout would raise the national flag at the morning routine parade to mark the start of the school's daily program.

Everyone would sing the national anthem, and the headmaster would make the day's announcements. Morning classes, then a break would follow this, then some mid-morning classes, a 1-hour lunch break, afternoon classes, and kids would go home at around three twenty in the afternoon. During the lunch break, most pupils would get out of class, go to the food shelter outside, pick up their lunch packets, and seek out a tree to sit under and have lunch. I did not carry a lunch packet daily. On the good days, I would bring a bowl of Githeri (Corn and beans) in my small Kiondo (small woven bag). Due to high temperatures and exposure to germs, the Githeri would go bad most days, and one could not eat it. On some bad days, ants would climb into the food and be all over it, making it inedible. On those days when I had no lunch packet, I would enjoy air burgers or grass. Of course, I would not eat grass, but one got a lovely succulent grass shoot, pull it out and suck the sap out of it.

You would do this several times until the bell rang, telling everyone that lunchtime was over. Coming to class late was taken very seriously, with the teacher punishing the pupil immediately, mainly by caning. We would find some specific plant, "Muhinga", that was said to have powers to make the teacher not cane you when you come late. You would tie a knot and put it in the back pocket. Knotted Muhinga would supposedly make the teacher not do anything even when you came late. Of course, this was not a fact, and it would only work sometimes, but we believed it and would do it daily. During my lower primary school days, after school, I would immediately get home, remove my school uniform, put on some casual clothes, pick up a pot, and go down the stream to fetch water for our kitchen needs. That was a routine, and I would go down the stream several times, alone or with others. I needed not to be told to do it daily. The disciplined way of doing things always made my mother proud of me. She could only praise me for my performance, thus elevating my self-esteem. My mother expressed this joy throughout her life, making me feel proud of doing something noteworthy.

In those days, you had to go for seven years of primary education to sit for the National Certificate of Primary Education if you did not repeat a class. Our geography teacher, Okm, was teaching us in class three or four at Ichaciri Primary School when he did something extraordinary. He was teaching us about the people of Kenya when he digressed and talked about the people of Sudan, a neighboring country. He then told the class that those people he was referring to were so black "like that one." He said this while pointing at me. Everyone in the class had a hearty laugh. From that day on, my nickname was "Negro", a nickname that I hated because it felt negative just because the class had responded by laughing at me. The nickname was used mainly by bullies to make me angry, and unfortunately, I always took the bait, making me a very sad primary school pupil. Now, I can joke about this, but it would send a burning bitterness inside me in those days. I think Okm was predicting that I would end up in America. I can only say this: He never realized how much he changed my life. I was praying to finish my primary school time as fast as possible. It, however, felt so long and was even made longer by repeating class 6 to give room for my older brothers, number two and three, to get a place to repeat the class after flopping in their standard seven exams.

Secondly, after failing my standard seven exams and not getting enough points to join high school, I repeated the exams and stayed in school a year longer. I remember the planned fights I had to fight to prove toughness following the persuasion of bullies, including my brother number two, nicknamed Gathimbu (a small fighting cane) because his fist strike was equivalent to a strike using a fighting cane.

I remember two significant fights that I had to do because the bullies would persuade both fighters with lies and say, for example, "So and so said you are so weak he can thrash you in a second!" The instigation by bullies was enough to generate a fight. First, it was my fight with Kagia on one day, then with Gaturu on another day. The bullies arranged the fights for two consecutive days during the 10 AM break. In my battle with Kagia, we earnestly exchanged blows until we messed ourselves up, both fighters bleeding from their noses. Kagia shouted during our fight and asked all bullies present to come and face this guy. "ukai tukiumbanire ithuothe," meaning "come so that we can gang up against him together" Kagia was admitting defeat this way. He said this as a teacher approached and dispersed everyone. My fight with Gaturu was swift, both parties exchanging blows in the first few seconds before he went down, declaring me the winner.

Our teachers enforced School discipline through strict actions, including caning, calling parents, sending pupils to detention after class, giving pupils tasks like running, etc. I remember one male teacher beating our asses off with specially prepared canes depending on the marks we received in Mathematics. The number of canes you received depended on the marks attained. I was an average kid, and so I got roughly half the number of strokes of the cane received by the poorest kid. Some kids got as many as 20 strokes of the cane, making school a small hell. Another female teacher used to cane us if we came to class late, and she would direct her cane strokes on the soles of the feet. Most of the kids had jigger-infested toes and feet due to not having shoes and due to poor hygiene, making most kids sad. My feet were heavily infested by jiggers, making me avoid kicking anything with my feet. The jiggers could not let me play any games. Soccer, a favorite sport in those days, was out of the question for me, and I came to dislike it.

We experienced many days of torture when the teachers forcefully removed jiggers from the feet of my classmates, especially those of one boy who suffered when they dipped his feet in a chemical called Kero or Kerosene, which had a powerful odor and irritating to jigger wounds. The teachers thought they were helping, but they were tormenting kids. Now I realize why I was so happy when primary school was over! It had been one hell of a ride. If you are not bright like most of us were, life was so hard you wished days could fly for you to leave this school. It was like the teachers were so intelligent, and we were so dumb.

It felt like the teachers hated us and would probably love us more if we had been more thoughtful. A case in point happened when they made one brilliant kid skip grade five and six to be in grade seven when he sat for the national examinations and passed with flying colors! His superb performance was great news for the school, and the kid became famous and went on to Alliance Boys' High School, the best high school in the country. This kid was a genius and was respected highly. In all those years of learning at primary school, we never put on shoes when going to school, and life was painful. You had to go to school but had no idea how to get organized and prepare for the national examination. The mind was not clear on the direction one was required to go. We did not get much help from our parents, and we had to figure things out ourselves. Most of the parents did not have adequate schooling to assist their children. The parents did not understand any of the taught subjects. These parents could not offer the pupils any meaningful advice about education except to stress the importance of education. It was up to the pupils to decide on their future careers with hardly any information available. In those days, most new teachers came into the teaching profession because there were open teaching job positions and not because they had a passion for teaching.

Furthermore, most of the teachers were untrained or were going through some teacher training programs. The teachers seemed distant from the pupils, and one would not expect the pupils to do well in school. The teachers were notorious for ruthlessly canning the pupils for very flimsy reasons. The teachers maintained high handedness in school administration as if the children were some form of opposition group and school life felt uncomfortable. The teachers would often ask the pupils to bring edible food products to class for learning purposes, but they would retain some foodstuffs for personal use. The exploitation of pupils also occurred when the pupils made nice-looking handiwork products that one would have sold to earn money for the school. The teachers were mainly concerned about disciplinary matters and general cleanliness.

They did not care too much about the school performance of the kids who needed to be inspired to work harder and reach greater heights in their pursuit of knowledge. The school performed poorly in national examinations; fewer than ten students would qualify to join an excellent high school. The churches controlled most primary schools in Kenya in my days. Ours was a protestant school, although I was a Catholic pupil myself. Sometimes, conflicts arose between these two denominations, and one had to stay on his side of the divide to avoid escalating trouble. We learned to sing protestant songs, which were lyrical and sweet. I also combined the knowledge of these songs with those of the Catholic church.

One favorite hobby of mine was reading. I mainly read novels and storybooks, which were so much fun. The reading would captivate me so much that I would forget where I was and lie to myself that I was in the place described by the author. Then I would realize I was still myself, not that superhero in the story. My hobby was fortunately co-shared by my friends Ngugi wa Keeru and Samson Kungu Kimani.

My friends used to call me King'ang'a (big Ng'ang'a), and I called them Gakugi (small Ngugi) and Gikung'u (big Kun'gu) respectively. They were both brilliant kids who loved to read and express themselves with the pen.

We would write stories and edit them for one another as if we were qualified professionals. Sometimes, we would read the stories aloud to one another, enjoying ourselves to the full. We all would seek available storybooks and share our enthusiasm with the team. The time to finish primary school soon found us, and we had to separate our ways and go to high school. We all went to different schools in different parts of the country. We promised one another to keep in touch and continue sharing the fun. Future writing and sharing did not work from this time because of the distances and the poor communication. We soon lost touch.

CHAPTER 4

High School Memories

Home living conditions had now improved. All our siblings had grown bigger; most were in high school. Our homestead was still in the same general area but had more houses. There was a main house constructed from timber and containing three bedrooms. My father, mother, and girls occupied a bedroom each. The girls lived with the youngest boys. Brothers two, three, and four had a bedroom each in two tiny houses built in the southern eastern part of the compound. Having my room was an outstanding achievement. I felt tremendous and grateful because my parents made it just before I became a man. My father had my house built during the transition from primary school to high school. It was a step-in life for me, and I had to go through circumcision and mature. Circumcision would also define my age group, which was given a name depending on the year of circumcision. For this, one needed a private room. On the day of circumcision, one would be taken to the local hospital at around 11 PM for the operation. A qualified person would carry out the operation. My first cousin, named after my grandfather on my father's side, was my godfather and was responsible for my adult education. He was also responsible for my protection against hazing from recently circumcised young men who were very demanding and brutal. The young men had some bad tactics of hazing, including humiliation, degradation, and abuse, which scared the newly circumcised individual. One had to buy cigarettes, which the young men would demand. It was a relief when the whole process was over, and my wound had healed.

The firstborn in our family was now married and had built himself an interlocked sisal wood house with two bedrooms some one hundred feet away from the main house. My room had a bed, a chair, and a table. I needed the chair and table to do my schoolwork. We would use a lantern lamp at night to provide light because there was no electricity. The miniature homemade lanterns were not good because they exposed someone to many dangers, including smoke with carbon monoxide. The naked flame, the kerosene smoke, and the smell were intense. The fire threat was always there, especially if one was not enjoying the chapter they were reading. I often dozed off and caught the lantern on its way to the ground. I was lucky my room never caught fire at any one time.

One of my brother's house accidentally caught fire this way. Many people had to come with water to put the fire out because that was the only way to extinguish fires in the area.

I was a hard-working student and enjoyed my time at Ituru High School. The school was just on the opposite ridge. You only needed to cross a stream called Kiabira to the next ridge called Ituru. I would go in the morning, learn at the school in the morning, go for lunch at home, then go for the afternoon session. I still remember those shoe marks that I would make running and jumping through benches made for our coffee trees to conserve water and prevent soil erosion. The marks would only show the heel or the back parts because I was recovering from jiggers that had infested my toes in my younger and earlier primary school days. I dared not step on the ground too hard as my feet and toes had grown soft from numerous attacks by different generations of jiggers. Jiggers usually embed themselves into the soles of the feet when walking. They are tiny fleas when they insert themselves in the feet through the skin. Once in the skin, they grow more extensive than their original size. The skin starts to feel itchy as the jiggers embed themselves even more profoundly. We would dig them out using safety pins. They are irritating and attract all your attention as you become more and more miserable. When inside feet, the Jiggers feed and breed there inside, and you can never have peace.

Ituru High School was a day school. Most students lived at home with their parents and would attend school daily. Most kids admitted to the school came from the area around the school. Living at home and learning at school was a very healthy arrangement because every day, I would enjoy fresh food cooked by my mother, who was very proud of me despite being such a demanding young man full of energy. My father was equally proud of me because he often met the school principal, who always told him how well I performed in class.

Having to stay home and not be in the privately rented dormitories like my fellow students was a significant advantage. I had all the time to study without looking for food, deciding which ones to buy, and cooking the food. Having ample time made my life almost perfect, and I performed very well in science and art subjects until it was not easy to decide if I would do arts or science subjects in my A-levels. I had very nice teachers who cared about how we were learning, and they would all show gladness if you did well in their subjects. One of the best examples of such teachers was a Christian religious education teacher and the school principal. He was such a great encourager; he would take my answers to examination questions as sample answers that he would use to teach the students in lower classes. He would also tell other teachers about me, and most of all, he was so proud of me that he would always tell my father about how great in class I was whenever he saw him. The other teacher with an excellent teaching style was a teacher nicknamed "Hiuka." He got this nickname because he used to walk swiftly. He was a Kenya Science Teachers' Training Institute graduate teaching Mathematics and Chemistry. He was a soft-spoken teacher who always paid keen attention to all the students and was happy when a student understood the concept he was trying to convey. He made me love Chemistry and Mathematics because he had excellent problem-solving methods. We all liked his teaching style, and many of my fellow students decided to study these subjects further.

My performance in this school was outstanding. My ranking in class was always below position number ten and would be one or two most of the time. I would compete with only one other student, and I came to beat him in the final examinations. When we were in Form Three, I was deeply encouraged when I received the highest overall marks in our class and got a book prize for the number one position from the Gatundu South member of parliament. I got the book Gulliver's Travels by Jonathan Swift, which made me feel very proud. By all standards, this was a blessed moment. The good Lord was at hand to bless this young boy who had no idea where he was going.

A typical school day would start at 7 AM when the students arrived and attended a parade between 7:30 and 8 AM. Four early morning periods of forty minutes each followed before going for a 20-minute break. After this break, periods five, six, and seven would come next, and students would break for a one-hour-long lunch break between one and two o'clock. After the lunch break, two more periods would follow, ending at 3.20 PM. The student preps came next, followed by a game period between four and five-thirty.

Missionaries of the catholic church started the school. During its inception, the school encouraged students to attend mass every Sunday at the Gatundu Catholic Mission. Like most of my family members, I used to participate in Mass at Gatundu Catholic Church. It helped me grow in faith and get a liking for religious study, which was also one of the subjects we were learning at the school. At the school, there was a building that I never saw in any other place. This building was called the ablution block, where students would clean themselves after sports or games. It looked odd in a day school.

I would visit some of my friends who lived in the student housing blocks and observe how they lived and cooked their food. They mostly cooked Ugali, and the pleasant Ugali scent was everywhere. In most blocks, the smell of burnt Ugali was overwhelming. You could quickly tell what they were cooking from the scent. The taste of the Ugali and Sukuma (kales) with Matumbo (chopped bowels, intestines) made by my friends was different from what I had tasted before. We would eat a lot because the food just tasted great. Githeri, a boiled mixture of maize and beans, was another typical food in the living quarters of most students. One would only perceive the smell of meat and rice in relatively fewer affluent students' rooms here and there. The fact that the students made their food was a great experience because they learned to be self-reliant and grow with some independence.

At this school, I loved to play volleyball and table tennis. Most of my school days were full and very busy.

The hard work finally paid off when I got admitted to a national school, Starehe Boys' Center and School, where I went on to study mathematics, chemistry, and biology. I got accepted to this prestigious school with another boy from my high school. God had found another opportunity to bless the village boy and move him to the City of Nairobi. We followed the footsteps of a brilliant student at Ituru High School who was one year ahead of us. I presented my four years of high school performance grades to the Director of Starehe Boy's Center and School, who immediately accepted and admitted me for two years of advanced level school to continue with education to prepare to join the University. My stay at Starehe was incredible. I felt accomplished because the school was famous and had a great name because of the students' outstanding academic performance in national examinations and the high standards of discipline.

The school was known for excelling in Kenya's national examinations, constantly competing with Alliance High School and other top-notch schools in the republic. The school was an excellent opportunity to meet and make friends with students from different Kenyan tribes (like my friends Paul Makau, Isaac Njoro, John Onuko, Polycarp Mandi, and David Maiyo) and Asians like my friend Arif Aziz. Being a student at Starehe made you a particular person who can appreciate other people from different communities, and one who can cultivate a humanitarian heart that seeks to give to others, especially when one received something in the early stages from someone else. At Starehe, I was a day scholar. I was a paying student who paid Kshs.800.00 per year. I would come to the school in the morning by Matatu or Kenya Bus Service (KBS) bus from Roysambu, study throughout the day, and then return to Roysambu.

At Roysambu, I stayed in a single room provided for free by my father's friend, who was working as a chef for an assistant minister in Moi's government. This man was a great gentleman who fed me like a minister. I lived there for about three months, enjoying excellent meals prepared for a government minister. The dinners supplied by the great Chef were rich in flavor and had interesting soups that changed daily. Most of the meals had nicely cut herbs that made them somewhat delicious. A fruity taste and aroma gave the food an unforgettable richness. You could hardly get enough, but I only had to eat what my bene-factor set on the small table in my humble abode that he had provided me without paying a dime. The Chef and my father had quite a great relationship. I would never ask the Chef for more food if I did not have enough, although my heart always yearned for more. The free dinners continued until one of the original Starehe Deputy Directors went to my home and did a financial investigation to determine how much I would pay once I became a boarder. After three months as a day scholar, I became a proud board-ing student. My acceptance as a boarder became a blessed moment for me! The time had finally dawned on me to enjoy life living in the school compound as a boarder. Therefore, I joined the club of eating "good," not getting satisfied, and looking for bread in the tuck shop. Bread from the tuck shop was our meals' most popular eating course. Bread always came last, and the satisfied student could go into the dormitory or class to finish the day's homework. I bet you can now vividly picture me at the tuck shop after dinner.

Everyone used to do this. One of my close friends would buy himself a quarter-buttered bread (The tuck shop worker spread butter on a quarter of a loaf of bread. The spread would be margarine and not butter, despite the fancy name. The bread would be higher quality than one with no spread). Less affluent folks like myself would buy half an unbattered loaf for quantity and price. This particular friend was great, and since we had joined the school simultaneously, we had much in common. He had grown up in the city and would take me out to his father's restaurant to dine out occasionally. Such a treat would be unfathomable for the village boy that I was! I would always look forward to such rare feeding moments. Remember how much I loved to have a good plate of "Karanga na Chapati" dish that was popular in those days in restaurants. His parents originated from Muran'ga district next to my parent's district of origin(Kiambu). I gained a lot of good experiences in the town with my friend showing me around. He knew his way around, having grown up here.

When I became a boarder, I joined Ngala House and this made me feel more like a Starehe boy than before. At school, we had inter-house competitions in sports and drama. I learned how to swim, and it was fun. I contributed to these competitions by running long-distance marathons for my house, Ngala House, and being a drama club member. I will never forget when I acted as a preacher in the drama competitions and warned my brothers and sisters to repent and turn away from their evil ways to avoid the wrath of God. My father and sometimes my brothers, like brother number two, would come to school to visit me once in a while and leave me with some pocket money to keep me well-fed. I counted that as a blessing and will always be grateful because it meant much to me.

We would receive three nutritious meals per day. We would get a hearty breakfast in the morning with some bread, tea, and fruit. Lunch and dinner were similar in presentation, but both meals were warm and freshly prepared. The kids in the lower grades were honored to serve food, and they determined what amount of the grab you got; otherwise, they would sometimes "shave" your plate and leave you unsatisfied. You do not joke with the lower secondary kids serving the tables and favoring their pals who would serve the following week. The bigger boys would need more food and had to have some money in their pockets (pocket money) to take care of themselves. However, I must admit that our food was first-class in taste. The cooks fried Githeri (a mixture of maize and beans) so nicely that it tasted so good you could not resist it. It would have some pieces of minced meat, which was a delicacy. You would start with an appetizer (a can of pudding), then the main course and a fruit dessert. The administration strived to satisfy the boys at the school or in the holiday camp.

I felt honored to visit a holiday camp in Mombasa twice while at Starehe. Getting an opportunity to go to the camp twice in my two-year stay in Starehe was a blessed moment for me that always made my heart throb with joy. The school owned the holiday camp, which was an excellent way for students to get to know the Kenyan coastal town. The camp helped students learn how to survive with other students outside of school and in a city setting.

We would go to the library to study and go to the beach. This kind of life in school on a camp made one feel great and proud to be a Starehe boy. The school instilled strict discipline in all students. Many prefects ensured that school rules were adhered to. One rule was revoking pocketing. You were not supposed to put your hands in your pockets and never leave any paper trash on the ground. If you find any paper or other trash on the ground, you should pick it up, or a prefect might notice you, and he would react against you either by writing you up for punishment or giving you a punishment there and then. It did not feel great if a prefect punished an older, non-prefect boy in a higher class.

You always ensured you did the right thing and looked around you to avoid any embarrassment. You did not want to be reported to the director for punishment because you risked expulsion. The most feared man in the school was the assistant director in charge of administration. You had to behave well around him if you were a Starehe boy. He also worked with the police as a crime buster. Those in the City who knew him feared him because he appeared everywhere a crime occurred. He was a high-ranking policeman in Kenya. My studies at the school were tough for me. Starehe is where I had to read extremely hard to prepare for complex mathematics, chemistry, and biology examinations. We had great teachers for all three subjects, but studying was tough. We had some brilliant students who would comprehend subjects so quickly that the average student was always left behind and needed to revisit the notes and labs more often. Of all my classes, the A-level classes were the toughest. God is great because I passed the A-Levels to join the University of Nairobi to study agricultural science.

Meanwhile, my younger brothers and I became creative and wanted to develop a language that only three of us could speak and understand. We only created a few words but could make exciting sentences and understand one another. The creativity brought fun and joy into our lives because we could communicate and share our thoughts, deceiving ourselves that nobody else could understand us. Language development helped us grow and appreciate many new words we would give to whatever we found interesting. It was easy for others to learn the language, but most people just laughed at us and found us quite weird.

CHAPTER 5
Found Myself A Lifelong Gig

A Starehe School student had many benefits that made
him proud to be part and parcel of this great school.
One such benefit was that Starehe had an old boys' hostel
where students who had completed school could stay while
looking for a job in the vast city of Nairobi. You only needed
to ask the director, and you would get a place to stay as you
search for a job. I was one of the proud and lucky students
who applied for accommodation and got it.

From the old boy's hostel to the city, one needed just a few
minutes to get to offices and hunt for jobs. There were both
temporary and longer-term jobs at the time, and we knew
where to look for which jobs. Some companies, primarily
manufacturing companies, needed day-to-day laborers, while
others trained workers for longer-term engagements. We had
cooking facilities in a shared kitchen and a hot water kettle
outside the rooms. You only needed to shout "Ng'ombe" in

the corridor to get the kettle, and the person with the kettle (not cattle) would answer and hand it over to you. The kettle was helpful in heating water for making some hot tea or coffee. In the shared kitchen, one could cook whatever meals they pleased. At this time, I had no cooking experience, and I opted to eat lunch in town, come home in the evening, make tea, and enjoy it with bread. I would travel everywhere in Nairobi from the hostel room, leaving job application letters and curriculum vitae with prospective employers. My first job was temporary at the Kenya Examinations Council, where we did some simple clerical work. The next most exciting job was working as an audit trainee at Peat Marwick Mitchell & Co. This was an excellent job where I learned accounting as I trained to become an auditor. An auditor is a person who reviews and verifies the accuracy of financial records and ensures that companies comply with tax laws. Auditors protect businesses from fraud, point out discrepancies in accounting methods, and sometimes work as consultants, helping companies find ways to improve their operational efficiency.

The audit trainee gig was a significant turning point in my life because I learned to work, and, more importantly, I knew how to play with numbers and audit and take stock of many things at my workplace and in my life. I used my time to learn new techniques in accounting and auditing. My love for company law also came out when I got a prize for getting the highest marks in the country in the Paper dealing with company Law 1 in the CPA1 KASNEB (Kenya Accountants and Secretaries National Examination Board) national examination. It was also a time to learn how to survive in the city alone, not with family or friends or familiar faces. Bad habits of drinking and smoking were to become part of my life easily. Such habits started slowly but quickly became part and parcel of my life. It is always a devastating aspect of a person's life as one struggles to fit in with peers who are also clueless.

Quitting these bad habits would have been the best way out, but youth pride has its way of holding onto a person and preventing them from seeing what is happening. As an audit trainee, I succeeded, and accountancy became a vital career. It was interesting how accounting staff in some companies would become so scared when auditors were present. Some were unsure of themselves, but the majority knew something would always be wrong with their work. Knowing they had not been extra vigilant in their work made them so timid that they would take off or be absent for long breaks to avoid scrutiny. It was a good time for me as a young man to feel so responsible as to find fault in work done by older, more experienced folks. Vouching was then the most crucial task, and it involved finding documentary evidence to see if it adequately supported entries made in accounting records. Auditing made me feel very important, and I had the money to match my bloated feelings. Work became fun, and I enjoyed every time I spent in clients' offices. I also enjoyed the after-work sessions with my colleagues. I had very understanding bosses who were brilliant instructors and trainers who went through every sampled document after another to satisfy compliance with accounting standards. I passed through the hands of professionals who greatly impacted my life.

I lived in a four-bedroom apartment in the Buruburu area of Nairobi with three other people from Starehe. These young guys had recently found jobs and started working in different industries. One worked at the Kenya Wines Agency; another was an auditor in another big firm. The third one worked at the Kenya Institute of Surveying and Mapping. It was interesting how we learned to organize ourselves to pay rent and share tasks like shopping and cooking. Sometimes, everything worked perfectly, and people did their chores as required, but a few times, someone would eat outside and come home drunk when it was his turn to cook and be at home. On some Fridays, we would all go out and eat together and then have some drinks.

We had quite a few drinking holes in the neighborhood, and more were coming up. As an Audit trainee, I remember earning more money than my counterparts who, at this time, were toying with teaching. For jobs in the industrial area, you would sometimes use someone's car to go to work but would get a handsome reimbursement. I was earning more than three times what my friends were making. The money was necessary in shaping my bad habits of drinking beer and smoking cigarettes, which became worse and worse with time. My bad habits later became one reason I would eventually go to the University to study rather than continue with this kind of life.

The drinking was excessive and was happening at every opportune time. My peers were all drinking alcohol and had the money to sustain the habit. It was a time to try out different types of drinks, including beers, wines, and hard liquors. My peers were very playful and would buy large quantities of beer and place them on the table, and sometimes, it was not possible to drink all the beer. You would have to struggle to finish it because your colleagues would order the waiter to open all the bottles to ensure you drank all the beers on the table. I was drinking the beer blend called Guinness and would often mix it with soda (Coca-Cola or Pepsi) to dilute it to avoid getting over-drunk. Dilution of my beer with soda helped to keep me sober for a longer time, but this used to offend one of my friends who wanted me not to dilute the beer, and he would always punish me by buying a crate of soda and ordering the waiter to open all the twelve bottles in the crate.

Such shenanigans would make the day very long. This same friend was also notorious for his smoking habits and had me hooked as a smoker and was smoking a packet of cigarettes per day. He would do many tricks with the smoke, including making rings that he would send around the room around the people. Smoking was still legal in bars and all public spaces then. Too much involvement with drunkards made me a little sick. I did not want to go to the village during vacations or weekends and would like to remain in the city. I remember this year's end, which must be December 1983, when my parents sent my younger brother, number five, to the town to come and plead with me to go home for Christmas, later in the month, to have a family get-together. My brother had a taste of the life I had and also stayed in the city until the holiday was over.

My friends treated him with goodies; he could not go home like me since he enjoyed himself. He, therefore, was unable to convince me to go home for Christmas. I worked at an excellent auditing firm that allowed me to travel around Nairobi, where most clients were. We also had clients outside Nairobi, like in the town of Eldoret, where we were auditing a garment manufacturing client. I made great friends at this firm and learned much about accounting, auditing, and management skills. This experience came early in my life and ended up being useful throughout my life. One fact is that proper financial management is significant to anyone, including people, homes, firms, schools, hospitals, etc. Everyone needs the lifelong skill of resource management for sound operational performance. I had achieved an essential skill that was of life-long utility.

Chapter 6
Becoming A Learned Friend

To prepare to join the University of Nairobi, I had to resign from my job at the audit firm. This decision was tricky because the two areas of interest were different. Agriculture and accounting seemed different, and I wanted to keep the news about my impending departure private. The other problem was that I had to join the National Youth Service before joining the university, and this was proving hard because I had become well-experienced in my job and was doing great. I resigned from my job at the auditing firm and traveled to Gilgil to start my service at the National Youth Service.

The service involved voluntary service while one was exposed to strict discipline, dedication, perseverance, persistence, courage, and commitment to higher ideals. We would wake up early in the morning, get inspected, and then go for the morning drills, which included running to the mountains. After an inspection in the barracks (where they would check whether your shoes were shining black, whether your socks were well positioned, whether the bed was nicely made and straight compared to others, etc.), challenging morning drills would start. The drills became too much for my body because I had been used to a better and softer life in the city. I did this for a week and became sick with cold-like symptoms. I saw a doctor who recommended that I leave the barracks immediately, which meant a great deal for me. I got to avoid the drills and return to my job. There was still a month or two before joining the university. I returned to the audit firm and worked there until it was time to enter the university.

Having decided to go to the university and study agriculture, I started a new life at the Kabete Campus of the University of Nairobi in April 1984. The entire course was to take three years. One would start with introductory courses in the first year and then get to the real agricultural material later. A lot had been said about agriculture being the backbone of the economy in Kenya, and here I was, ready to get the necessary knowledge to play my role as an agricultural officer. In those days, each student would apply for a student loan through the higher education loans board. The board would grant the loan and disburse payments to the university to cover the costs of student accommodation, dining, tuition, and library fees. The individual student would receive an upkeep allowance, which the students called a boom. Students lived in halls of residence on campus, which felt great and well organized.

I stayed in the Soweto Hall of Residence, sharing the room with my future brother-in-law.

One of the fears one had was to live with a person of another tribe or someone who could not understand you. You would curiously look at your roommate and wonder what language to use. We were lucky to be paired up with promising students who were very friendly, and it did not matter what tribe they were. They were all very friendly and cooperative and guided by their quest for knowledge. They came from all corners of Kenya and were eager to start their studies. Soweto Residential Hall was far from the other residence halls, and one had to walk through a paddock with an electric fence. As you walked to class, you could get enough time to revise your notes between the paddock's two gates, not forgetting the fresh air. On the way back from college to Soweto, one would go downhill and remember all the day's events, having an incredible feeling of accomplishment. The food at the dining hall was always great, and we would even have some unique dishes like Chapati once or twice a week. I appreciated all that we got. Sometimes, the students went on strike and claimed that the food could have been better, but this was because they became spoilt and needed to remember where they came from. The university released the student boom every three months. Despite the small upkeep allowance, it was vital for the students because it felt like a big deal.

Students from my class would take a bus in groups of friends, go to local bars and downtown Nairobi, and visit famous watering holes like Sabina Joy. Next to the campus were many bars in Ndumbu-ini and Uthiru, where most students found themselves when they were rich. Everyone would have a great time. The boom lasted only for a week for most students with no discipline. Some students returned to class when all the boom was gone. I had a particular group of friends with whom I shared a lot of comradeship during our studies. These friends came mainly from my Agriculture class, but others were studying Food Science and Technology, Range Management, and Veterinary medicine.

We formed study groups with these friends, enjoyed beer, and participated in their private family matters whenever anything concerning arose. These friends were composed of some individuals that were big in build, others medium, and others were smaller. We used these categories of build to show respect to one another. Although we were young, we would refer to one another as an elder. The Agikuyu name for elder is Muthee. We would combine the medium and big individuals into one category and refer to them individually as Kimuthee, meaning the prominent elder. Kamuthee, the minor elder, was the name given to the smaller friends. These salutations remain in force to date. Now that we have become elders, we appreciate one another similarly. We show our respect this way and believe that we have something great with which to enjoy one another even when so much water has passed under the bridge. The agriculture course was a broad study area, with many classes involving introductory and applied science courses. One had to work extremely hard to pass well to graduate. Students were very hard working and spent much time in the library. Some highly professional professors were very dedicated to ensuring students performed well in their areas of study and did so much to encourage us. The professors were graduates of international universities who had studied in highly distinguished universities. As the studies continued, some of my friends and I formed study groups that helped us a lot in preparing for examinations that one needed to qualify for the degree. This good background enabled us to do very well in the examinations. Forming these study groups was a crucial part of my development. I got to know many people who played a significant role in my growth as an agriculturalist and, more so, as a plant breeder.

Sometime in 1986, we moved from Soweto Hall of Residence to the newly constructed student accommodation unit near the field station. We moved in together with the same roommate I had at Soweto. It was during this time that I was blessed to meet my wife. She had come to visit her brother, who was my roommate. It was late, and circumstances forced her to spend the night. We both quickly developed some great chemistry and talked the whole evening, going into nighttime, discussing many general issues in life. Little did we know that we were to become life partners later. While learning Agricultural Science, there were two mandatory farm practice attachments in large-scale and small-scale farms. For the large-scale farm practice, I went to a dairy farm in the Rift Valley, where they milked the cows using a machine and grew several crops. In the large-scale farm practice, I was privileged to have the company of my best friend at the college, who later studied Agricultural economics. For the small-scale farm practice, I went to a small farm in Western Kenya for a month, where they produced some crops and had dairy cows under a zero-grazing system. I graduated in November 1987 with an upper second-class honors degree. In September 1987, I started a Master of Science degree course in Plant Breeding. In this course, we studied this art and science that uses fundamental principles of Genetics and Plant Breeding to improve important plant traits for the benefit of humanity. This Course was essential in my life.

During the course, I made significant decisions that influenced my life path. From September 1987 to July 1988, we did the coursework. Thanks to my Professor, I planned and started my research project concurrently with the coursework. The first year involved taking courses in Plant Breeding. I passed these courses well after putting in a lot of effort. I continued with research geared towards understanding Pigeon peas' adaptation, comparing the improved varieties to existing ones.

Pigeon peas are important legumes grown in arid and semi-arid areas in tropical and subtropical regions. Working with Pigeon peas was an excellent opportunity to travel to different parts of the country where Pigeon peas are grown, including the semi-arid areas of the Kenyan coast and the eastern provinces. We had research projects at Kabete,

Thika, Kiboko, Kibwezi, and Mtwapa. I learned how to drive a car at this time. The Pigeon Pea project driver gave me a couple of lessons when we were out there on fieldwork, and before long, I could drive a car on my own. I did not obtain a license at that time but waited until I acquired my vehicle. My professor was amiable and supported me with all he had. He put all the project resources at my disposal to help me succeed.

He guided me in developing all my research strategies and techniques. He was a brilliant plant breeder, and I knew I had the guidance of the best teacher ever. He was very hard-working and always on the move, looking for new breeding ideas for the different sets of crops he worked with. He knew how to start new projects in breeding other crops and was great at sourcing funds from local and international donors.

My professor had research projects in different parts of the country depending on the crop of interest. In some of my professor's research projects, I established the projects by planting the seeds, taking care of the plants, collecting data, and harvesting. I worked with a research assistant, a project driver, and a small crew of about five people. The relationships among this research group were excellent, and we all felt great working for my professor. We were like a family, and we were all very close to the point of introducing our spouses or best friends.

I got excellent cooperation from the Department of Crop Science staff until the end. The staff were accommodating in many situations. They would help obtain the materials and supplies needed during field and laboratory research activities. They would facilitate students in securing research funds. Their help went from research work activities and thesis preparation issues to typing and printing the thesis. My research work on my Master of Science in Plant breeding was completed in 1989, but I graduated in 1990.

CHAPTER 7
A Committed Agriculturalist

Around June of 1987, we knew we had passed our examinations and were to graduate as Bachelor of Science in Agriculture graduates. We immediately started looking for jobs in the Ministry of Agriculture and Kenya Agricultural Research Institute (KARI), hoping to get entry-level positions. I was successful in early August of 1987 when I was employed at KARI and posted to the Thika High-level research station as an agricultural research Scientist. I was instantly allocated to fruit research and immediately hit the ground running. Within the first few weeks, I had already met a great strawberry farmer and familiarized myself with field conditions.

During this time, I lived in my house in the village and would travel by matatu from Gatundu town to Thika, from where I would take any public vehicle going beyond the research station. During my travels, I already had some colleagues from near my home who worked at the station, making me feel like I had good company. We would take the commuter taxis together and look out for each other. Employee comradeship is a common occurrence where fellow commuters become good buddies. We would even occasionally share a beer at our final destination (Gatundu town) from work. Before I could settle down and get to know my fellow researchers and get acquainted with research, I was re-admitted to the University of Nairobi to do a Master of Science degree in Plant breeding. I had to leave employment to go back to study. I was awarded a scholarship from the German Academic Exchange (DAAD) for my excellent performance in my Bachelor of Science degree in Agricultural Science, where I scored upper second-class honors. Similar scholarships were awarded to a few other graduates in different study disciplines.

The research station job was a short engagement, and I gained only minor experience. It was an excellent opportunity to meet some great agricultural researchers at this station who have contributed significantly to horticultural science in Kenya. I benefitted from the helpful scientific discussions we had. To study plant breeding, I had to pass through the hands of very experienced and internationally recognized professors, like Paul Kimani, Mukunya, Ayiecho, Kimani Waithaka, Gupta, and Tyagi, among other greats of the time. The professors worked hard to teach the students and conduct advanced research in their areas of study. Our professors worked hard to guide and encourage us to contribute to research and science by writing articles in scientific publications. Some of them were pivotal in fostering critical thinking and ensured that our intellectual development was at par with international standards. The professors were also responsible for evaluating student performance. They would collaborate with colleagues in other national and international universities to stay in touch with the current developments in their areas of interest. As a Master of Science student, I lived outside the campus in Ndumbu-ini in a shared room for a few months before living at the Mugabe Hall of Residence, where postgraduate students lived. At this time, I upped my game in cooking for myself and living independently. This was when I had to choose the kinds of meals to cook, the most reasonable quantities for one person, and for which period.

In the summer of 1988, around August, my best friend and I decided to visit the city of Mombasa. We invited another one of his friends to give us company. We took a train and were in Mombasa in a few hours. On the coast of Kenya, we invited my wife-to-be to join us and become our tour guide because she was born here and had lived here for years. We enjoyed the food and the many things the coast could offer, including walking along the extensive sandy beaches, collecting sea shells, visiting the crocodile farm, and knowing the city and its environs. This trip was another excellent opportunity for me to appreciate my wife-to-be. We had a lot of fun together, affirming our commitment to one another. This long journey was another blessing since it marked a significant step in coming closer and getting to know each other better. Our friends would later confess that they were taken aback by our getting together, especially when we met for the first time, and both friends observed that both of us licked our lips repeatedly on seeing the other person, indicating the significant effect we had on each other. These magical things must have happened by the grace of God when we looked into each other's eyes, sending messages to our brains to acknowledge our strong attraction. Another significant encounter with my wife-to-be happened at her brother's wedding ceremony towards the end of 1988. I had gone to the wedding, and I was in charge of my professor's project pickup truck that my professor gave us to help transport the bridegroom's parents. In the evening after the wedding, we drove towards their rural home in the rain, and we eventually got stuck in the mud before reaching the house. The people walked the rest of the way home, and I had to spend the night in the cold with my driver. In the morning, we struggled to remove the truck from the mud. It was not a four-wheel truck, making it quite challenging to pull it out.

Furthermore, there was no other vehicle to use to tow the truck. We had to pay people to lift and push us out of the mud when the pickup truck reached a muddy hole on the road, and there were many such holes. We eventually got out of the woods and returned to the city. This adventure helped cement my relationship with my girlfriend by getting to know her family, although not officially. We continued to communicate by phone and mail, becoming more committed to one another and making promises for future cooperation. Communication was crucial because both hearts were getting fond of each other and needed consolation. Continued great rapport led to more meetings and serious decision-making. Increased understanding was essential because of this unsigned agreement to live together and become husband and wife following the Agikuyu customary law. We agreed that we lacked the finances to have a wedding ceremony, but we imagined the possibility of marriage in the church at a future date.

The Agikuyu community has a delicate dowry process that involves some regulations to be followed before the groom is allowed to marry the bride. The dowry process is called Ruracio and calls for a series of meetings between the two families. Both parties underwent a series of negotiations to determine the bride price. The families on both sides are supported by men and women of their clans, together with family friends led by respected elder leaders. My father selected Francis Kariuki to represent my side of the table as spokesman and invited a few other Agikuyu elders (Athuri) from my area to join my delegation.

My bride informed her parents that she had found someone interested in marrying her. Her parents inquired about their clan and formed a team for negotiations. On the first visit, I visited my bride's family with my team to identify my bride's clan (Muhiriga). Traditional rules do not allow intermarriages between certain clans. It was decided that an opportunity existed for a marriage between us. A second visit date was set for my team to visit my bride's home to know their home (Kumenya Mucii). On the appointed date, my team visited my bride's homestead with traditional beer (Njohi ya Njurio) to ask for her hand in marriage.

After enjoying many delicious foods and refreshments, my team spokesman announced the purpose of our visit. After some introduction, the elders had a conversation on the issue, and the lead teams on both sides were invited to get to a secluded place to have a private discussion about the matter. There was some agreement that we could go ahead with our plans. A third meeting date was set when my team would return to my bride's homestead, and I would officially book the bride a ceremony called "Planting the tree branch" (Kuhanda Ithigi). As required, I delivered live animals, Mwati (Ewe) and Harika (small he-goat), for the ceremony. The bride price was negotiated "Kuniruo Miti). We were to pay a certain number of livestock valued in cash terms. That day, we started paying the bride price with what we had (hiding our goats or Kuhithia Mburi in the Agikuyu language). Later, we arranged another visit, but it became a little demoralizing because we did not have sufficient cash to leave at the bride's homestead. My bride's team told me I would not be given the bride until I paid the dowry. I went away a little disappointed but determined to look for funds and return at a future date to complete the process so that I would be given my bride's hand in marriage.

CHAPTER 8
Research Scientist On The Move

On the 6th of March 1989, I joined the Coffee Research Foundation (CRF) based in Ruiru as a coffee breeder. I was living in the Mugabe building at the Kabete campus of the University of Nairobi. My wife had just decided to marry me. She had joined me in my single room at the college, and we were ready to start our lives together. We decided to introduce our families and start our traditional marriage negotiations. We set everything in motion. We felt comfortable living together, hoping to pay the dowry slowly as we moved forward.

To go to work, I would travel by public means first by bus to the Nairobi city center, then to Ruiru town by Matatu (Minibus or minivan), then take a CRF staff bus to the research station. After work at 5 PM, I would follow the reverse route. I would be exhausted at the end of the day. My wife would also take a bus from the Kabete Campus to the Nairobi city Center and then take a bus or minibus to Thika. She would equally be exhausted at the end of the day, and we would spend some money this way just for transport. We had to change this trend. After two months, we moved to the CRF housing, and we got a vast 4-bedroom bungalow, which felt quite huge for two people. We also had lots of areas for gardening and empty spaces.

We thought we were still not ready to settle down here because we would soon get our firstborn. The move to CRF removed my road movement and reduced my wife's previous journey by half. Towards the end of the year, we moved to Thika so my wife could be closer to her workplace. We lived in a one-bedroom apartment in Nyaka Court. Our first-born son was born in early 1990 at Gatundu Hospital. When my wife felt ready to bring the child into the world, I took her to Gatundu, where I knew she would get help I could not provide. Getting our firstborn son was a great blessing because it turned my wife from a girl to a mother. This became a cause for me to celebrate with food and refreshments with my extended family. We would grow kale and vegetables like Managu (Solanum nigrum) and Terere (Amaranthus) near our apartment building in Thika. The vegetables did very well. At this time, I would travel to work by commuter taxi to Ruiru and connect with the CRF staff bus at Ruiru. I took a car loan and bought a pick-up truck to venture into the transportation business.

I then started driving school classes to obtain a driving license. Within two weeks, I was a driver and I could drive a motor vehicle here and there. The aim of the truck that I obtained through a car loan at my place of work was to transport goods for people and charge them a fee. Transportation of cabbages from Njabini in south Kinangop to Gatundu had appeared quite lucrative. Still, it did not end well because you would need to either get into the business and sell cabbages yourself or rent out the vehicle to several customers, which also was not working well.

Transportation of bananas from Gatundu to the markets in Nairobi depended on customers that were going to those markets. When we moved the vehicle to Thika, we would position it in the "Ask for Transport" area and wait in a queue until its turn. The business was not progressive and had trust issues that made the owner distrust the driver. A few months later, the truck was involved in a bad accident, which I would rather forget. This accident negatively affected our lives and nearly made us destitute. Life became quite tricky due to the low salaries that we were earning at the time. We were living a vicious cycle of eating from hand to mouth. By the time you get your salary, you have accumulated debts equivalent to and, in most cases, more than your earnings. Having a personal car was a dream that you dared not dream. Then comes a deadly accident with multiple lawsuits thrown your way. At this desperate time, I had no one to turn to for financial support. My father-in-law was the only person who could lend us some Kshs. 5000.00 that we needed to deal with the lawsuits. The lawsuits were coming because the insurance company did not want to compensate the passengers despite the comprehensive insurance coverage.

The insurance investigator from the company where I had insured my vehicle came to investigate the accident. The investigator gave a biased report that was unfavorable to me, stating that the accident truck was mechanically defective. This report made the insurance company refuse to honor genuine claims on this ground, and their decision was final. The written-off vehicle took much money to put it back on the road. Relatives of the diseased passengers filed court cases in the High Court of Kenya to sue me for the insurance dishonored claims. Had those lawsuits prevailed, I would have gone to jail for years because I would not have had the millions of shillings they were demanding.

Our second son was born at this challenging time. He was born in the Aga Khan Hospital, one of the CRF-recommended Hospitals. The way I took my wife to the hospital was quite interesting. We went to the commuter taxi station and talked with the driver of the seven-passenger minivan. He agreed we should rent the Minivan to take us to the hospital before dropping off other commuters. So, the Minivan had other passengers who should have been informed about the plan to go to the hospital first. The other commuters made much noise when they realized the driver had taken another route to the hospital. We felt anxious at the other commuters complaints but were happy when we got to the hospital and got help immediately. Our son was born soon after. This was a blessed moment occurring at a trying time. The good Lord had given us yet another grace at a difficult time. During this period, circumstances forced us to borrow money for daily living. We were able to repay my father-in-law's debt a few months down the road. It would have been terrible if we did not repay because we still owed him a lot. I had not completed paying my dowry. On my travel to work journeys from Thika to CRF, I would sometimes get rides from two gentlemen who also lived in Thika. These gentlemen were the chief accountant and the chief administrative officer at CRF.

The rides were quite a relief whenever I was lucky to get them on the roads, and I would be home earlier than usual. These two gentlemen were settled individuals who had worked for a while and had the means. Sometimes, it is great to have individuals like these who can make one smile even when life is complicated.

As life became tougher, we moved from Thika to Gatundu, my home and birth town. We had built a three-bedroom house there. We hoped we would live in it and receive an owner-occupied house allowance, which was better(more) than an ordinary house allowance. I had started building this house using the boom I would receive in college. The house was a source of great pride because only some students did anything substantial with their boom. Most of them finished it in the drinking places scattered everywhere. The reality of moving into our home happened, and we moved in. We would even grow our food crops, including bananas, corn, beans, and potatoes, as well as cash crops like coffee, avocadoes, and mangoes.

We had many great experiences on our little farm. We reared a calf, which grew into a heifer and became a milking cow. We had bought the calf from a friend at CRF. We were selling excess milk at restaurants in Gatundu town. Living off of land would be quite a relief because we would only use money from the sale of food crops and milk to buy those grocery items we could not produce ourselves. The funds we saved would allow us to buy a quarter kilogram of meat to make our meals as tasty as we wanted. It was always a great feeling to be able to buy that quarter kilogram of meat because our children loved to have the taste of their food improved using meat. I was also a big fan of meals with meat that tasted many times better.

These savings would also help me to buy goodies for the children who were growing very fast and would ask me to bring back "Mandathi ma ha Ndune na Passina," meaning "bring back for me the famous Kenyan baked product called "Mandathi" from Ndune' s restaurant plus a Passina which was a packet of juice popular with our kids. Ndune had a restaurant that used to make Mandathi the size of an elephant's ear and was popular with the old and the young people. My wife would walk 2 KM from home to work, and I would commute from Gatundu to Ruiru by bus or Matatu and connect with the CRF staff bus. The distance from Ruiru town to CRF was about 10 KM, and one could not walk that distance. At Ruiru, there were other means of transport, especially when the staff bus was in the garage or could not be available. I would use public means of transport, either by taking a Matatu or a bus. Any staff member who owned a car and knew me would give me a ride if he or she wanted to.

The other alternative would be if you are lucky to be found by a random CRF vehicle driving back to the station, and the driver happens to know you. When you went by public means, the bus would drop you along the main road, and you would have to walk into the station, which was 2km inside and away from the road. It always helped if one had a companion to walk with. You could either follow the tarmac, on which, if you were lucky, you got a vehicle giving you a ride to the station, or follow the shortcut. To go faster, most people would pass through a sometimes muddy path, which was a shortcut but exposed you to dust, mud, or falls. One had to reckon with weather conditions like rain and dust. There would be rain sometimes, and the shoes would be covered with muddy red volcanic soil or dust whenever it was dry and windy. On some great days, I would get a lift from one great gentleman who owned a motorbike, and we would ride between CRF to Gatundu town through shortcuts and be home before you knew it. Riding with this gentleman was my preferred means of transport, but it depended on the generosity and availability of my friend. Riding through the back roads was fun, and one got to know the places better.

Of great importance is the experience with tribalism and how one has to remain focused despite having connections with tribal leaders who are bent on keeping their own in office and who promote tribal-based machinery for running institutions. Tribalism was a terrible experience, especially regarding some of the research directors at the time. One director was from the Luo tribe and was the director of research who was the director at the time of my appointment. I remember him for supporting his tribe mates, who were my senior and junior officers.

He was also the director who approved my Ph.D. studies on condition that the Foundation covered my boss's doctorate study costs. According to my recollection, our director was the kind of man who could allow tribal insubordination to happen many times to support people of his tribe. Two of my junior officers' most memorable incidents involved the following actions.

At one time, one of these officers ordered a lower cadre staff to supervise casual laborers to uproot and discard over 500 cuttings of my experiments with cuttings in my vegetative propagation research to establish the effect of rooting hormones on the rooting of coffee softwood stem cuttings in the study involving cultivar Ruiru 11. My head of department reported the matter to the director of research, but this only made matters worse for me as I was now required to see the director and explain why I was not cooperating with my junior officers. This same junior officer did not learn any lesson because he again destroyed an experiment with grafting experiments, and the director did not discipline him but ignored the matter and moved on. Such frustrations made life in the workplace very difficult.

I remember even some disappointment from another one of my junior officers in charge of the computer and our data entry geek. For a research officer to use a computer, one had to go through a gentleman who was always busy with the only available computer, making it so difficult to make use of it. Learning to use a computer or analyze data took a lot of work. Because he was working to please my boss, he always reacted with so much unease that one always felt unwelcome. He would make sure you knew who he was and who he worked for before you could use the computer. He also seemed to enjoy frustrating more senior officers who were usually post-graduates. Yet, one needed to use the computer because it was such a rare commodity, and a department was lucky to have at least a computer.

Getting permission from this gentleman was very difficult because he had some girls around him who served as data entry clerks. He was a man of women, and you can imagine the kind of smile he would give you to show you disregard. It was a relief when cybercafes started operating at Kenyatta University, and I would go there whenever I wanted to use a computer. Time was also unfavorable because this was when computers were becoming the thing for everyone. The boss would typically allocate you the research areas at the station with little money. He would give his tribe members the money-making assignments, share the proceeds with them, and give them excessive powers. They would sell seeds of the new variety Ruiru 11 to farmers and not issue them with official receipts because the seeds were in great demand, which outstripped the supply.

The boss would ensure he was there with his best lieutenants, who oiled the cogs of the money channels that ensured their survival. I was allocated the vegetative propagation area of research at the breeding department, which was at that time an unlucrative area of study (until the board gave it a lot of money to revitalize it to make it produce millions of seedlings, a feat that was to happen in my leave of absence). I had some success in this area, though, and one can follow my papers on rooting softwood stem cuttings, grafting, and top working of Ruiru 11 in coffee journals. The job was a turning point in my career because it became my gateway to international travel and studies. Between March and July 1992, I attended an international course in Plant breeding at the Wageningen University in the Netherlands.

It was the first time I stayed away from my family for an extended time. I endured the loneliness and enjoyed my time in another country. It was my first time boarding an airplane. When I went to the Netherlands, family and friends took me to the airport to see me off. They were very excited about my overseas trip, sang songs, and had refreshments. They wished me well and hoped I would do well out there. I came back after four months and was happy to be received back by the same group of people. It was a great feeling to be received by your people with song and joy. When I came home, I brought back some new and old clothes for my family. I also brought back a music player with a radio, a cassette recorder, and a record player. I got a small saving of about Kshs. 30, 000.00, which we used to install a solar panel and do some electrical wiring for our house. I was fortunate to go for my doctoral studies at the Humboldt University in Berlin with full benefits and went to Israel for a biotechnology course. I also went to Ethiopia to learn about integrating new technologies with farmers' knowledge. My wife and boys lived in our house near Gatundu town from late 1991 to the end of 1994, when they joined me in Germany. As for me, I had to go to Germany in 1994 to learn the language by undergoing a six-month course before starting my Ph.D. studies in 1995.

When my family joined me in Germany in 1995, we lived in a student housing apartment in the Wedding area of Berlin. We were there from 1995 to 1999, when my studies ended, and we had to return to Kenya. I had been on study leave during my studies and was required to return to Kenya and work for CRF. My employment at the CRF was also the most critical platform on which we applied for the USA Green Card lottery. The Senior coffee breeder position at CRF was my last position in Kenya before migrating to the USA. I have tremendous memories of work-related joint activities with my friends at the CRF. We worked hard in our respective departments to advance research on the coffee plant to bring new technologies into the industry. We also had a good share of fun. We enjoyed outings of roasting meat (Nyama Choma) in various joints, ate cabins (boiled goat heads) in goat butcheries, and got drunk like there were no tomorrow. A close friend of mine who is a dental assistant would sometimes join me in our drinking sprees. The strange thing was how I would give him a ride on our way home, and would wait for him to extract a tooth from a patient so we could get some money for drinks. In such cases, we always hoped that the patient would have all the needed cash.

CHAPTER 9

Wit Sharpening Overseas

I was a coffee breeder working to develop new coffee varieties and improve the coffee plant. The most important work at the station involved multiplying the coffee variety, Ruiru 11, through every means possible. We produced seeds through a well-organized seed garden. Some of these seeds would be allocated to farmers by the CRF board. We would germinate some of these seeds to produce seedlings, which would be grown and made ready for distribution to farmers as seedlings. We raised other seedlings by rooting softwood stem cuttings of Ruiru 11. Yet other seedlings were produced using grafting. In grafting, the scion is Ruiru 11, and the rootstock is a pencil-thick seedling of a variety adapted to Kenyan coffee growing conditions like SL28 or SL34. My work focused on research on the vegetative propagation of Ruiru 11. I had done considerable work on rooting softwood stem cuttings and grafting seedlings of traditional varieties with scions of Ruiru 11.

I also did significant work on topworking coffee trees on plantations. I loved my job and was quite successful in it. I was still looking for ways to improve myself academically and looked at the possibility of further studies abroad. I searched for such opportunities in Kenya as well as outside the country. The admitting institution should have provided a scholarship to cover tuition, accommodation, and out-of-pocket expenses. Education is an expensive affair. Most of my applications to schools of higher learning were in the United Kingdom, Australia, and the United States. Most of these applications were unsuccessful because the schools would give an admission letter but not offer scholarships.

Between March and July 1992, I attended the 22nd international course in applied plant breeding in Wageningen, the Netherlands. My head of department had participated in the 21st international course in Applied Plant breeding, making this an inherited opportunity. It was a crucial course because the earlier coffee breeding program leader was from the Netherlands and had established a great network between his country and coffee breeders at the CRF. The Dutch government organized the course as a part of the then-development cooperation program with Kenya. The Dutch government had funded the coffee breeding program earlier and made significant strides in developing coffee varieties.

I went for this course to improve my knowledge of Plant breeding and become proficient in it. The course focused on methods to improve the genetic makeup of plants to develop improved varieties. The course involved many aspects of the art and science of genetics, plant breeding methods, variety development, hybridization, selection methods, mutation breeding methods, etc. All subjects were fascinating and very useful for all students attending because these students were representing their home country institutions. The professors teaching the course were from the Wageningen Agricultural University and were very smart and knowledgeable. They were also very friendly and engaging.

The course structure was well organized and had many valuable lectures, practical laboratory sessions, and field trips. The trip treat was a special one, done in a comfortable bus with a chaperone explaining everything as you travel. It felt nice to be involved in these trips. During the field trips, we had an excellent opportunity to see and appreciate the significant advancement in Dutch agriculture in green-houses and the fields. We were awed by the many fruits and vegetable crops that were growing in plenty in greenhouses and big farms. It was terrific how crops could be grown using automated greenhouses supplied with water and nutrients controlled by a computer. Cucumbers, paprika, and tomatoes were excellent in growth patterns, numbers, and colors in some cases. We also learned about land recla-mation, where the government reclaimed the sea to make farmland. The trips we made to Amsterdam were educative as well as captivating. There were also exciting field trips to the country's north that had much to learn from. At the end of the course, the teachers gave us an examination for those students who wanted to do a Master of Science degree in Plant breeding later. Although this examination did not eventually turn into a master's course, it was very satisfying and motivational to me. I received the highest marks in most subjects and was the best student.

We learned some aspects of the diverse Dutch culture, listened to folk music and dance, danced, and appreciated classical music and works of art and architecture. Of course, one had to appreciate the Dutch wooden shoes, or clogs, designed earlier to protect the feet of farmers, factory workers, and artisans.

While taking this course, I met a great German professor who was one of our professors. This man made a difference in my life! I approached him one day and asked him if he knew any plant breeding professor in Germany who could accept to supervise my doctoral studies. I explained that a sponsor would offer me a scholarship to study in Germany if I could get a supervisor. He said he would recommend one, and he started to contact him on my behalf. The German professor agreed to be my supervisor and started writing letters. The professor in Germany was the head of the biometry department at the Humboldt University in Berlin and was willing to supervise my doctoral studies without any conditions. This professor was Erhard Thomas. I had for a few years known that the DAAD, the German academic exchange service that had sponsored my Master of Science degree in Plant breeding course at the University of Nairobi, was willing to support my Ph.D. studies if I could get a German professor willing to supervise my studies. The good Lord was again on my side, and I had found myself a professor! In 1993 Prof. Thomas visited Kenya, and we identified a relevant study area. Since the coffee breeding program had amassed data on different elite breeding lines over years and locations, this would become the backbone of my genotype by environment interactions studies in coffee.

Interaction studies are essential because similar methods could be followed in the future when trying to understand the adaptation of varieties to differing agroecological zones. During his visit to Kenya, I was happy to give my professor a grand tour of the country using transport facilities available to me at the station through the courtesy of my boss. We visited some Coffee Research station fields in substations and the Tsavo National Park, the Nairobi National Park, the Snake Park, and the Rift Valley. There was, however, an incident where some thieves snatched my professor's camera and handbag with his passport, and we could hardly catch them. The German Embassy was very helpful, and they swiftly got the professor some travel documents. Soon after this visit, DAAD approved my scholarship, and I was to go to Germany to start my doctorate studies.

First, I had to prepare myself by attending the University of Bremen and taking a six-month German language course with other international students. After this, I traveled by train to Berlin and started my studies at the Humboldt University of Berlin. Although I had learned the language, it was challenging to overcome the language barrier. Most sales associates in shopping malls were uncomfortable speaking English for fear of making mistakes and would not speak any English. After arrival in Berlin and with other students, we searched for shared accommodation and spacious apartments because we hoped to be joined by our families. My family joined me after overcoming a few hurdles in getting a visa and the German academic exchange confirming their support. I had to travel back to Kenya to arrange for my family to join me. Eventually, it all worked well, and we found ourselves together again in a foreign land. Being joined by my family was an outstanding achievement every person of our caliber would have wished for. We all hoped this would make all the difference in knowledge for me and my family members, who would get better education and better opportunities in the future.

It was a big step in moving from a developing country to a developed one. I moved the family to a new apartment in a student housing block in the Wedding district of Berlin, much closer to the university, located a few train stations away at Invaliden Street in Berlin Mitte. Our children were very young, being three and four years old. They were attending a kindergarten in the same neighborhood in the morning hours.

They would then go to the Daycare place adjacent to the school. Daycare attendants would bring them to the school and get them after school. My wife would pick them up at five. Our children enjoyed going to the Daycare place and the school very much. They were swift in learning German and soon became our teachers because we were still not yet fluent in the language. The boys became taller and brighter every day, learning as many new tricks as possible in a land with many school resources. They learned how to ride bikes; showing them how to do it was fun. They were very good at puzzles and games. They also learned how to swim, and they were doing very well in competitions and would bring trophies home.

My wife also attended a six-month language course, which we found necessary for survival. Since my visa was a student visa, my wife was not allowed to work or study. The foreign affairs office argued that she had come to accompany me during my studies. They threatened to send her home to reapply for her study visa, and we had to drop the visa request. We had seen this as an opportunity for her to improve her education by taking an advanced course in nursing, but she was not allowed to do this. Being a hard-working person, my wife got some cleaning jobs in houses owned by several German clients, some of whom were friends. She worked for these clients from the beginning of her stay in Berlin to the end.

She would get the key from a hidden place, open the door, clean and dust the apartment or house, then return it to its place and take the agreed-upon amount of money left with the key. The funds she made were significant because we needed as much money as possible to manage ourselves and help our families back home. We also needed funds to pay the dowry my father-in-law's clan needed. We saved enough money to send to my father-in-law to contribute to the dowry required.

Earning some money on the side was a significant achievement in our lives because our debts would slowly get paid and remove those guilty feelings that continually reminded us of our shortcomings. The Lord had been faithful in transforming us from debtors to lenders. We could now afford to send money home and assist needy folks. We would help parents by sending them money for their upkeep, and we could contribute if required. At one time, we sent all my brothers and sisters some Kshs 10,000.00 each for personal use. One relative neighbor had negative comments when he learned that we had sent everyone this money, saying that it was too little without even knowing where it came from!

My wife found the little earnings from cleaning houses exciting because she could now go out and work, and the money would be enough to buy her a new dress or buy me a new shirt or something for the boys, and there would be some change left over to buy some food items. Getting extra earnings had never happened before, and we found it very resourceful. Besides, it was an excellent way for her to spend the day because I would be at the University, and the kids would be in Daycare. She would also go shopping for our requirements and get groceries for our home. On Sundays, we would attend mass at the American Church in Berlin, an English-speaking catholic church where we were privileged to meet and know many international people.

On this day, we would also find time to go out and play with the children. It was also a day to eat the Turkish Doner Kabab prepared at that street corner near an underground train station. It was as if the Kabab was begging customers to come in and enjoy the hot meat or chicken wrapped in a special bread. Many customers would come in to get a Doner Kabab on their way home. We loved it so much that we would go for it every Sunday after Church. Sunday was a great day to spend on tourism. We visited many note-worthy places in Berlin and its neighborhood, including the German Bundestag (Parliament), Brandenburg Gate, Tiergarten Park, Alexander Platz TV tower, and the Berlin Wall remains, to name a few places.

We used public transport to move from place to place. Public transport in Berlin is well organized. Public transport includes different modes of transport, including the S-Bahn, Subway, Buses, Trams and ferries. My family and I mostly used the S-Bahn and the Subway. During my stay in Berlin, I studied most of the time. On some weekends, my family and I would join other Kenyans in parties organized by the Kenyan community to observe national holidays. At such times, we would share and enjoy great foods prepared by Kenyans from diverse backgrounds and different walks of life. It was a great time for everyone; we enjoyed and laughed. We shared great stories and experiences, which were very interesting. We heard stories about racial discrimination based on people's skin color. We told of how some Germans touched our children's hair and wondered if the hair was authentic or fake. Germans from the eastern part of Germany thought black people could wash out the oil on their skins. The Germans believed these Africans were white and had applied oil on their skins. Others wondered if Africans came to Germany by plane or by ship.

Another assumption is that people in Africa live on trees because of the lack of houses! Someone said he told the questioners that it was confirmed that people in Kenya live on trees because they have no houses. He told them that even the German Ambassador in Kenya occupied the best and the thickest tree. He said that this was a conversation-ender. Some would talk about how they managed to come into the country. Many of them had made friends with German tourists on the Kenyan coast, and these Germans helped them get a visa to travel either as husband or wife. Only a few were students. Others had come as Au pairs and were enjoying their experiences.

My professor was a warm-hearted, sharp-minded, and wholesome individual who sincerely cared about my work as his last student. I found him proficient, patient, and nurturing when working with him. In our department, he treated everyone in a friendly, exuberant, and empathetic way. Although he was our boss in the department, he treated us all equally, and we all felt accepted. As a teacher, he took me to many historical agricultural institutes in his car and enlightened me on their significance in Germany and world agriculture. We attended significant plant breeding conferences and regular biometrical research meetings for all department members. He took me out on trips meant to teach me about German culture, enriching my general knowledge and understanding of historical and geographically important places in Germany. There were also some trips to parks, buildings, cities, etc., of monumental value. We visited parks and palaces in Potsdam that were very interesting from a historical point of view.

To my family, my professor was a fatherly figure who stood out as this generous and compassionate person eager to share his resources with his family and ours without passing judgment. My professor loaned me enough cash to bring my family from Kenya to Germany without worrying about when I would repay him. When I felt comfortable enough, I refunded him this money several months later, but he still wanted me to repay him much later. He treated his family members in the same way that he treated mine. Every year, he would invite my family and me, together with all his children and their families, to his home in Potsdam.

He would neatly arrange sets of goodies and presents he had prepared for everyone and set them in a corner. All the presents would have someone's name. All families, including mine, would retreat to their allocated corners and enjoy their goodies after enjoying a delicious dinner. In the meantime, we would enjoy great music from the piano or an instrument played by him, his gifted children, or his equally gifted grandchildren. His wife, Regina, would then show everyone the bedrooms where they would sleep for the night. The following day, he would drive us back home.

He treated me as a friend, not as a student. It was like he saw something I did not see in myself. He always offered me the best assistance to answer my questions and went out of his way to show that he cared about my work. He would go to great lengths to ensure I got all I needed to make my studies successful. He would even send me to other professors if he felt they had something to offer, and I would go directly to these professors and learn new data management and analysis techniques. This man greatly impacted my life and my family by adding value to our lives. He tried to make us as comfortable as he could. We felt comfortable in his presence and knew he was on our side. He understood the difficulties of coming from Africa, not being in our comfort zones, and having to deal with some individuals who never understood black people.

While studying, I would do light manual jobs to supplement my stipend and support the family better. I would do most of these tasks on weekends and during weekdays after studies at the university, going up to midnight. Some jobs involved helping people when they were moving or relocating.

An employer would hire you to move heavy and delicate items like the piano, shelves, wardrobes, etc. Another job I did for about six months was that of a cashier in a beverage store. I worked as the cashier for returned empty bottles, where I would receive the empty bottles mainly in cases from the customers and give the customers receipts.

The customers would then go on and collect whatever new products they wanted to buy and then go and give them to the cashier who dealt with the sale of products. The cashier would then refund the customer the money, or he would deduct the receipt for the empties from the total bill. I was doing very well and loved the job. They paid me well, too. I worked on this job for a couple of months until my family visited me at work on their second day after arriving in Germany. They were so excited about learning that I had some way of making extra money on the side. I did not know that family was not supposed to give you a visit at the workplace, and I got fired immediately. The firing happened despite my excellent performance, which the manager and my co-workers had previously praised me for. I believed there were personal reasons that made the manager fire me. The manager was an unmarried lady and would probably not cope with the fact that I had a loving family. Other jobs involved loading or unloading all sorts of items depending on whether an individual or company gave you the job. For some jobs, you would go for one day, and they tell you they need you for a week or longer, and you would accept if you had the time.

My other jobs involved washing dishes in restaurants or working as a sales associate in a shopping mall as a sales agent. I did one such job in a restaurant for almost one year and became a professional dishwasher in a lavish, elegant restaurant in the western part of Berlin near Kurfurstendamm. The folks there loved my work, and I enjoyed the evening shifts. I had a great time with other students on this job. A professor of one of my student friends gave him a surprise visit by coming for dinner in the restaurant one day. It was such a shock for the students, although the professor understood that we were not getting enough money as students and we had to supplement our incomes.

I also did part-time work for a year as a sales associate in a French shopping mall in the middle part of Berlin, where I became very knowledgeable in the geography of France by knowing which wine types came from which region and what characteristics were specific to these wines to make them stand out. My team and I worked in a bar setting, and we would serve customers who were very excited after visiting our stand, and they felt like we perfectly understood their needs. The added benefit of this job was getting to sample most of the expensive wines to know their outstanding attributes and describe the wines to the customers. I could not help feeling great at this job; it stands out as something I enjoyed doing. I remember the boss who supervised us in this job due to his openness and the knowledge he would pass on to us to be productive in our work in the department. We had a team of students studying different areas of study at various universities. For these jobs, it was essential to balance studies and work.

Chapter 10
Resettling At the Homeland

Towards the end of 1999, I completed my studies and graduated. Thanks be to God! I had managed to be first again. What a blessing for a person from Africa! My family and I began to prepare to leave Germany. We had always known that our stay was temporary and that a day was coming for us to move back to our roots. Our children were unhappy with us because we were removing them from what they knew to the unknown. We had to give them a few treats to convince them that it was for the best and that we had no other option but to fly back to our homeland.

After all, CRF was still my employer and needed me back because they had given me a paid study leave. We put our belongings together and found them too many and too heavy. We decided to ship the overweight belongings using a cargo freight. We were able to get a good deal. We arranged such that our belongings would arrive in Kenya almost at the same time as we did. I was back at work at the CRF and was ready to serve the nation again as a more learned fellow.

I had a responsibility and was required to serve my employer. The rules required me to serve my employer for at least two years before I would think of another employer. Settling down was not easy initially because life in third-world countries is always more challenging after living a life where almost everything is guaranteed. The kids had become fluent speakers of the German language, although they still could speak Kikuyu fluently. They needed these primary languages, English and Kiswahili, to cope well in school and the community. The teachers would interview them and fail to understand them because they could only express themselves in German, and the teachers were not at ease because they could not understand even a single word. Due to this shortcoming, there were difficulties in getting the two boys admitted to the good public schools we wanted. They found a private school willing to accept them and started the learning drill. The academic performance in the first semester was abysmal for both of them, with the poor kids leading from behind. Then came the second semester when both kids had a median performance, having advanced very quickly. In the third semester, their performances were excellent, obtaining class ranks below number ten. They were now at par with the other kids in their class and could reasonably compete with them.

Teachers soon came to love the boys for their outstanding academic prowess. Ruiru 11 was the new variety of coffee developed at the CRF. It had better quality characteristics than existing varieties, and farmers in all coffee-growing areas of Kenya needed it in large quantities. It was resistant to the primary coffee diseases. It had higher yields than the traditional varieties. To contribute to meeting the demand for Ruiru 11 and make extra money, I established a coffee nursery at Gatundu where I would grow seedlings of Ruiru 11 from seed for sale to farmers in my area. The nursery did not make a lot of money but was able to keep us going. One event concerning this nursery occurred one day and made a difference. The day was April, the third day of 2002. On this day, early in the morning, a large-scale farmer from the area came in to buy coffee seedlings. He bought seedlings worth Kshs. 70,000.00. I could pay for two Nissan mini-vans that ferried us to Nyeri for our traditional marriage rite of Ngurario without any complaint. That same morning, I went to the post office and found a letter announcing my wife had won the green card lottery, allowing her to take our entire family to live in the USA. That was a significant occurrence because it would change the direction of our lives. We traveled to Nyeri that same day to celebrate our traditional marriage rites. The ceremony involved my wife's family and mine sharing food and drinks with visitors from both sides.

All people were to become witnesses who would attest that my parents-in-law had given their daughter's hand in marriage to me. This ceremony, a part of my traditional marriage ceremony (Ruracio), is called Ngurario. This

119

ceremony marked the completion of our dowry process. The ceremony was significant because my bride became part of my family. I consider this day the most blessed day in our journey with my wife because many blessings came to us all in one day.

Having arrived home from a foreign land, I had to be ready to utilize my vast knowledge of biostatistics and plant breeding research. I settled well at my place of work and was more respected. I was called a "doctor" by all at work. The new work-related accolades gave me an incredible feeling of blessing. We did not return to live in our house in Gatundu because it was deficient in several ways. First, it had no electricity, so we could not use any of the entertainment equipment we brought back. There was no piped water, and one had to depend on rainwater, fetch water from a nearby stream, or buy water with drums from Gatundu town and transport it home. Then there was the security issue. Our area was not very safe in the village, mainly because it was prone to attacks by thugs known to steal everything. People would have known we were back in the country from a far-away land. People were inclined to imagine that you would be carrying lots of money, and they would most likely want to visit you. We tried to avoid anything that would have brought challenges into our lives. We did not want a situation where we would have to fight unnecessary battles. We found an apartment in the Mjengo building in the Thika town center, where we decided to stay. The apartment had two bedrooms, a kitchen, and a sitting room. One bedroom was ours, and the other was for the two boys. The apartment had a balcony with a half wall made of stones and protected by a metal grill. The boys had a bunk bed. The balcony was an excellent place to enjoy some sunshine on weekends and watch vehicles pass in the street a block away. Our lives had now changed, and we were having some little savings that we were planning to use to better our lives. We could now afford a car, and we bought one. When purchasing the car, we got assistance from a broker a friend introduced to us.

He said he was a friend, not a broker. He made extra money from us in the car deal through price misrepresentation. Because we were in a hurry and very trusting, we paid for the car but later realized that we had spent more money on it than it was worth and much more than the owner's sales price. This experience and others taught us to be cautious with people, especially brokers. We could now drive ourselves from place to place in our car. I could take my wife to work and my children to school. Being able to help others was a remarkable transformation.

I was now the one to give others rides when needed. I would park the car at the nearest gas station in the evenings. I would pay the guard a little money to watch the car at night. We still had our gas cooker, so we felt we had most of the necessities for a good life. We still had our old fridge and now had a washing machine, although connecting it to the Kenyan water system would be challenging. We could afford to take our two boys to any private school we could get. We were much better in our social standing than before, and people showed us respect. Being accorded respect was a big deal for us. Before we went to Germany, people did not notice our existence as a family. This time around, we seemed to matter. On weekends, we would drive to Gatundu in the morning and do some work there or visit relatives. We would then return to Thika in the evening. We decided to construct a rental building in Gatundu near the catholic church because we already owned the plot there. Our decision to do this was well-informed, although we did it grudgingly. We had tried to acquire new plots, but every arrangement would end badly, with someone planning to con us. We got into trouble when we were going to buy some land in Kibirigwi. We were lucky we met a good Samaritan who told us not to go ahead with the deal because the land had multiple title deeds. We also attempted to buy a plot in Thika town twice and discovered that our friends were working with the brokers to make huge gains at our disadvantage.

Our friends were very greedy, and we stopped them from helping us look for land or a plot.

Sometimes, the prices would double or triple overnight if the brokers learned we had just returned from Germany. We generally found the land brokers' agents very dishonest and untrustworthy. Every time you had to get a property, they would come in droves and compete for your money even when they did not have the correct documents. When constructing the rental building, my wife managed the site and did very well in sourcing the building materials and payment of the construction crew. An experienced contractor correctly drew the building plan. We had a good plan, and a foreman was there to start work after following the procedures laid down by the county building department.

The foreman was a local builder with experience building story buildings in the town and Nairobi. He came to us, recommended by many people who had seen samples of buildings he was involved in constructing. The foreman brought the building masons based on how he knew their work in other projects. Other building crew members were day laborers from the local community who came to ask for work and could follow simple orders from the foreman. There were shops up front facing the road, and one-bedroom and two-bedroom apartments planned from the shops towards the back. The crew constructed the foundation, septic tank, and soak pit quickly. Next came the basement building blocks. Then came the ground-floor shops and apartments. Then, it was time to do electrical and plumbing work. The doors and windows were to be of stainless steel and glass. A local metal contractor won the bid to make doors and windows, beating four other bidders. He was happy to do the metal grills where there were stairs and corridors. We had challenges with the plumber. As the construction was going on, we went to Thika town one day to purchase building materials. We met a mature-looking man buying plumbing materials. He introduced himself as a plumber, and our first impression was positive. He looked like an honest man, probably because he wore a turban, and we thought he was a man of God who could do the job. We had been looking for a plumber for some time.

After deliberations, we agreed to let him come to our site and give us an estimate. He indicated the materials he would supply and their specific quality in his estimate. He also stated the money he needed for his labor. We settled on a total bill of Kshs. 100,000.00 for him to do all the plumbing work from start to finish. When it was time to start the job, he came and began with a crew of two people. In the next two weeks, plumbing work went very well, with the crew coming daily. On different days in these two weeks, the plumber would come to me and ask for more and more money, and he took all the Kshs. 100,000.00. In the third week, the plumber told me he had used up all the money and could not afford to buy more pipes, taps, connectors, couplings, adapters, etc. He said I would have to add more money or purchase the materials myself. I gave him another ten thousand shillings to buy materials. I would go out with him to the market and realized that the materials he was collecting to install in our building were defective or did not meet the quality standards we had agreed upon. It meant that he had already broken the terms of our contract. He would also fail to appear on site on those days we agreed on and stayed for weeks without saying a word. We decided not to cooperate any further with him because we kept losing more and more money, and lots of plumbing work still needed to be done. We needed someone consistent. We, therefore, told him not to come to our site because we had decided to look for a different plumber. Due to the debt he now owed us, we decided to hold his toolbox as collateral, although we knew he could not refund any money. The toolbox was of little value and contained only a few tools.

Confiscating his toolbox angered him, and he reported the matter to the police in Thika. He misrepresented the truth, lied to them that we had stolen his toolbox and building materials, and hid them in our house. The police quickly issued me a warrant of arrest stating that I would be arrested and brought before a court of law to answer charges of theft of goods belonging to the plumber. The matter made me very worried because I feared dealing with issues concerning the police. Such an issue was a lie propagated by someone trying to bring trouble when he was supposed to have done a clean job and gone to another job. In Kenya, people can easily manipulate matters, making things complicated when they are pretty simple. Police are known to take drastic actions on simple issues, and depending on what the accuser has said or even paid, the police officers can stretch a small issue very far.

After contemplating for a while, I went to the Gatundu police station and presented myself, and the police gave me two police officers to come to the site and understand the case. The policemen advised me to introduce myself at the Thika police station. I went to see a family friend who was also an influential politician. He attentively listened to my story and asked me for all the details. Sarcastically, he said this was the beginning of my wealth troubles. He wrote a note, sealed it, gave it to me, and told me to take it with the warrant to the Officer Commanding the Police Division (OCPD) in Thika.

The following day, I went to see the Thika OCPD, who called the policeman who had written the warrant of arrest. The policeman came and quickly said the plumber had given him a little money to write the warrant, and he also said he was not going to follow through with the warrant, which was only supposed to threaten me. The OCPD asked the policeman if there was a way of getting hold of the plumber. The policeman said it was possible because the plumber had just left the station. The plumber was near, and he quickly came to the OCPD office. The OCPD asked the policeman whether that was the man we were discussing. The policeman answered in the affirmative.

The OCPD told me to forget about that plumber and work on my house with other plumbers because this was known as conman. He was having more than five cases where he had defrauded people of a lot of money. Many people had reported the man to the police station, and the police had ordered him to pay the people he had conned, but he could not do it. About two weeks later, this same plumber again went to a clerk from a law firm and had him write me a threatening letter saying he was to go to court in seven days if I did not return his goods. These problems occasionally come up to us and hinder us from going forward in a world where dishonesty is a common threat. We continued building the rental building until our funds got depleted. The funds got depleted before we could bring in electricity. We had to ask for a bank loan to pay the power company and teamed up with two other neighboring plot owners to have the power company bring an electric current to our premises. The electricity installation would cost each of us KShs.240,000, which was a lot of money then. This money was only a third of the funds needed to bring only one post for the electrification of three buildings. We were lucky all three owners could agree and look for money for this purpose. I made a poor decision by buying an old truck, hoping it would reduce the building costs associated with material delivery to our construction. I also wanted to become a building materials supplier if all went well. I bought the lorry with our last 1 million shillings. The truck was a used Isuzu tipper truck that was a dumping truck, the type of truck that has an open body that is capable of tipping and dumping material.

It could transport diverse materials, including sand, building stones, gravel, etc. I should have thought better before buying this truck. The advising mechanic should have advised me correctly. The mechanic thought it would be an excellent investment, and this made me bold due to having him on my side just in case of breakdowns. My wife did not support this plan, and it turned out to be a money guzzler because the truck perpetually broke down and always needed a lot of money to bring it back into operation. At first, I looked for a driver in Gatundu town and got a young man who was very determined to let the truck become useful. We decided to use the tipper truck to deliver sand from the sand-rich areas of Kitui and Machakos and bring it for sale in Gatundu and the surrounding areas.

The truck had limited movement due to limited building activities in the area. The little movement made us think of taking it to Thika, where we lived. This way, I would monitor the truck operations, and this area had more construction sites.

This business picked up, and several of my friends started ordering sand. The orders by friends and colleagues were bad debts because my friends and colleagues at work would order sand and not pay for it, and if they paid, it took them a while to pay and only after a lot of persuasion. The bad debts made the business fail to realize any substantial gains. There was also frequent crankshaft trouble with this kind of truck. We kept changing the drivers and crews to revitalize the business but this did not work. Some drivers were too bright for me. They would work very hard and bring back several truckloads of sand daily. They would sell it to customers but report to me only part of the day's job earnings. They would note only two deliveries and keep the money for the other two trips if they went for four visits. Some days, I would go far to take spare parts to the truck if it broke down far away. I would also pay for the dinner and accommodation of the crew if the tipper truck broke down far away. I would pay for their meals until we came back home. Matters with breakdowns never became better, and we continued to take losses. We were happy when we finally decided that the truck should not bother us anymore and decided to prepare it for sale. We repaired and parked it at a mechanic's garage, waiting for a buyer. We advertised it and stayed for over six months. The only customer who came after six months bought the truck at a meager price of two hundred thousand shillings, leading to a loss of eight hundred thousand. It was such a huge loss.

We had plans to use the money we got from selling the truck to acquire a plot in Ngoigwa in Thika as a memorial property. We looked for a plot to buy, and one of our friends found us a potential plot that we only needed to see and pay for. At this time, we learned about my wife winning the Green Card Lottery to migrate to the United States. Winning the Green Card changed our plans, and we decided to use the truck proceeds to support our migration to the United States, which would be the next phase of our lives.

When the construction of our rental building ended, my wife started a shop for cosmetics and women's beauty products. We should have gotten a license for a pharmacy, which had too many requirements. One had to find a qualified pharmacist who would take responsibility for the chemist shop and put his pharmacy license on the line. The pharmacist we knew did not agree to assist us. Since we knew no other pharmacist, we decided she should start a cosmetics and beauty products shop. She sold hair care products at the shop, including hair wigs, extensions, shampoos, conditioners, treatment and masques, hair driers, clippers, trimmers, etc. She also sold makeup products for eyes, face, lips, etc. She also sold skin care products, bath, and body products, among many other products. She would travel from Thika to Gatundu every morning.

Then she would sell products at the shop for the whole day up to 6 PM, then travel back to Thika. Gatundu was a small town, and the products sold at the shop would appear expensive for the local ladies. They would opt to travel to Nairobi or Thika to meet their needs. The sales at the shop were relatively low. My wife worked at the shop for about one year. She started feeling like that was not the right fit for her. My wife decided to return to nursing when the beauty shop business failed to perform better. She applied when the Ministry of Health advertised for nurses nationwide. The ministry invited her for an interview at Nyeri. I took her for the interview, driving all the way. In Nyeri, she was lucky to find two people in the interview panel who took particular interest in her. One was my cousin, and the other was someone who knew and had worked with her brother.

The job interview turned out to be positive. We drove home a happy lot, and before very long, she got a letter of acceptance to rejoin the Ministry of Health. The ministry stationed her in Enosaen in Narok County. The county was over 500 KM from home, and we did not want her to go to work there. We started looking for a way. The county is far away from Thika, where we were living. Getting her back to Thika became challenging because the rules of engagement required that she served for at least one year at the station. She would go to work and come to see us after a couple of weeks, which was not a good idea because I could not manage to bring up the children alone. I tried to involve political activists to help her get transferred. Using politicians was the hardest thing to do if you were an ordinary person like me.

The political operatives demanded lots of money to have senior politicians get involved. The method failed to work, leaving me devastated. Little did I know that better days were on the way. A lady colleague who worked at the CRF deputy director's office looked at me one morning when I went to collect a document from the deputy Director's office and saw my sorrowful face. She asked what the problem was. I explained my problem with the transfer and described the rigidity of the rules at the Ministry headquarters. I also explained that I had talked to senior officers at the Ministry headquarters, who said getting a transfer was impossible. The lady colleague was very sympathetic and went into deep thought. After a few minutes, she said she had found a solution. She offered to introduce me to her cousin, who worked at the ministry headquarters. I thought it was a joke, but she was earnest and immediately called her cousin. I explained to her what I needed. The cousin said it would be possible and I should go to her office that afternoon. That was God right there performing miracles! I told myself, filled with disbelief. Another blessed moment!

That afternoon, I went to the Ministry headquarters and met my colleague's Cousin. She took all the details of my wife, and told me to come to the headquarters the following morning. The next day, I was in her office, and she took me to her boss's office. I could not believe my ears when the boss lady asked me where I wanted my wife posted and when. Hearing positive news caught me unprepared because I had given up and also came to believe in the impossibility of anything positive happening. The lady realized that I was surprised by her question and asked if Thika was the appropriate answer to the first question, and immediately, was the answer to the second question. I nodded in the affirmative, and she handed me the letter of transfer.

That evening, I went home, prepared my boys, and told them we would get their mother and bring her home early the following morning. At 4 AM, we were awake and prepared to start our journey. We went to the bus station and took a minibus to Nairobi, where we got onto a bus to Kilgoris town, where we took a minibus to Enosaen. It was a Friday, and my wife could not present the transfer letter to the boss at the health center; she had to wait until the following week when she would also hand over her duties to the next person. The boys and I traveled back on the weekend because they needed to return home to attend school the following Monday. For us, this whole transfer issue was a significant accomplishment as this had presented a challenge that appeared impossible to resolve. We were glad my wife returned home to work in the local hospital.

We also learned a lesson that people assumed to be relatively insignificant could play a significant role in life.

We would only have had the transfer we needed because of people in lower positions. My wife's experience working in Enosaen was not much because of her short duration there, but it was rich and educational. She came to understand the way of life of the Maasai people and a little bit of their culture. I enriched myself with the experience of cooking different balanced diet meals for our children and being more organized in performing various necessary tasks while running our home alone without my wife. This kind of experience was critical. It was, unfortunately, the kind of experience that became fuel for neighbors to talk and spread falsehoods, claiming that my wife had left me. The reason for the rumors was that people only saw me with the children most of the time. Such rumors originate from the paternalistic Kenyan culture, which makes people think it is not correct for a man to take care of his children without his wife.

CHAPTER 11

A Short Visit To the Holy Land

I had always dreamt of visiting Israel to see the kind of place it is and to fulfill my heart's desire to see the place where Jesus was born, brought up, and preached. Over the years, Israel has emerged as a robust economic powerhouse in the Middle East. Due to this development and the rich religious history, many people, especially Christians, dream of one day traveling to Israel. In 2002, I visited Israel for an international course in plant biotechnology at the Hebrew University of Jerusalem at Rehovot, funded by the government of Israel. Israeli Agency for International Development at the Ministry of Foreign Affairs (MASHAV) organized the course for people working in developing countries.

The course organizers aimed at promoting new biotechnological techniques in modern agricultural production. I obtained a certificate of attendance. Attending the course was an excellent opportunity for me to study and walk in some places Jesus walked. What a chance to move closer to God it was! The trip was priceless because every Christian dreams of it! I appreciated learning the history and cultures of the peoples of Israel and was grateful for this experience, which equals no other. I learned to say "Shalom" when greeting someone or saying goodbye, an important salutation meaning complete peace and wholeness. We went to the Church of the Holy Sepulcher, or the Church of the Resurrection, built in the fourth Century. While inside this church, I felt the adorable scent of the perfume that Mary had used to anoint the feet of Jesus to prepare him for his burial. According to the Bible, Mary took a pound of ointment from Spikenard, which is very costly, and anointed the feet of Jesus and wiped his feet with her hair. I brought some bottles of blessed water from the river Jordan, where Jesus's baptism by John the Baptist occurred.

I distributed this water to friends and family to bless their homes and properties as well as themselves. River Jordan has a rich history, and many miracles are said to have happened there. Water from the Dead Sea has been researched and found to have a low content of pollen and other allergens. People would get into the dead sea and bathe for health reasons. I also returned home with some Dead Sea skin and arthritis therapy products. I brought back some Dead Sea mud, which is rich in minerals and is said to relieve osteoarthritis. We visited the Masada, a stone fortress high above the Dead Sea on a rocky Messe.

The Jews highly regard this due to telling a story of resolve and resilience. In Jewish history, the Masada was the last fortress before the Romans overtook Judea. In the story, a hundred Jewish rebels fought to their death against eight thousand Roman soldiers. When the Romans marched to victory, they found only two women and five children who took their lives rather than let the Romans enslave them. I visited the City of Jerusalem and went to the garden of Gethsemane at the foot of Mount of Olives. According to the Bible, Jesus went through agony in the garden, prayed there, and was crucified here after being arrested. We also saw the Wailing Wall and the Golden Mosque in Jerusalem. The Wailing Wall remains to date from the second Temple of Jerusalem, which the Babylonians and Romans destroyed. It is the most religious site in the world, where Jewish people traditionally pray and lament on Fridays. We saw the Golden Mosque in Jerusalem only from a distance. It is on top of the site of the second Jewish Temple.

We could not go to some places like Bethlehem and Nazareth because these towns were volatile places that were not peaceful to visit at the time. It was a chance to make friends with people from different developing countries who also attended the same course. One great friend made in Israel, Bosco Bua, came from Uganda, remains in touch, and is an excellent acquaintance. The course was very significant for us because there had been major biotechnological advancements that we needed to catch up on.

We had excellent professors who were outstanding in their presentations. Learning new biotechnological techniques was some welcome knowledge. Seeing the many agricultural advances in Israel was also interesting. It will remain a memorable time because I had exhausted my funds when constructing our first rental house in Kenya but could not raise enough money to bring in electricity. I had taken a bank loan of Kshs. 240,000.00, that took a long time to repay. Two other neighbors and I contributed Kshs. 720,000.00 to install a single electric post to supply us with electricity for our three buildings. The allowances I got during this trip helped me repay that loan in full. It was miserable that the interest rates charged on loans in Kenya were too high and prohibitive at that time because people's salaries were too low.

Chapter 12
Africa My Beloved Continent

Africa is my home continent, where I was born, raised, and prepared for the world. Given the opportunity and time, I can write much about the continent, but I will only mention the few places in Africa I was blessed to visit in my few adventures. Traveling to another African country sometimes occurs when we go across borders. We do this by driving or walking and rarely by flying. I have had to cross the border on foot to go to Uganda at the Busia town crossing point to buy cheaper African materials for making African dresses. I also did some window shopping there for electronics once. That was only in the past because the prices today are similar to those in Kenya, and there is no distinct advantage to going across. I have crossed the Tanzanian border several times at different places on foot or by car just out of curiosity. I only got one opportunity to fly there once.

In 2002, I attended a short course on Integrated and Participatory Approaches in Biodiversity, Plant Breeding, and Seed Production Systems held at Awassa College of Agriculture of Debub University, Ethiopia. The Netherlands government supported the course. Participatory plant breeding is the process by which the farmers and other stakeholders participate in a plant-breeding program, with opportunities to make significant decisions during the whole process. In this way, breeders similarly utilize indigenous and improved germplasm in breeding programs. Researchers get a chance to consider the needs of the marginal and poor farmers. In this process, the selection of locally adapted germplasm is emphasized instead of broadly adapted ones. The process helps to address and learn about the plant biodiversity in this country, which is the center of origin for many crop species. It was a great learning experience because I saw and heard diverse bird species singing and making noises in their natural environment, which was unpolluted by the use of pesticides on monoculture cash crops. In the colonial days, minimal colonial influence in Ethiopia left plant and animal diversity unadulterated. Some bird species are exclusively found in highland forests and shrubs in that region, for example, the Abyssinian catbird. I learned much about Ethiopian culture and was amazed at some plants that exist only here and as food crops, including Ensete and Tef grass.

Scientists consider Ethiopia the center of origin of many field crops like coffee and Tef. The coffee plant and coffee culture originated here. Ethiopian traditional dancers danced for us and sang Ethiopian music that involved a lot of shoulder and neck movements, which was amazing to watch. It was fantastic to see horses in some regions of Ethiopia, and local people said that the horses originated here and not elsewhere. The horses were used for public transportation and were a sight to behold.

I had a chance to visit South Africa in 2010, a few months before the 2010 19th FIFA World Cup matches. The visit occurred when I worked in the United States as a Plant breeder for a seed company.

I visited a seed company in South Africa that was marketing seeds from the company I worked for. First, I flew to Kenya, where I stayed for two weeks before flying to Johannesburg. I spent my first few days in Kenya, visiting and greeting my people. In Kenya, I had a minor business event trying to clear some peas sent by our company in the USA to a client. The Kenya Plant Health Inspectorate Service needed more seed production information to release the seeds. I described the USA's growing conditions to the officers, who then allowed in the seed when they were satisfied with my explanation. In South Africa, I attended a meeting of farmers and interested parties at my host company. I participated in ensuing discussions and found the meeting a great learning experience. Before leaving South Africa, I did some shopping for my family. The shopping was exciting, considering my constant conversion of dollars to South African Rands. I had to use my judgment to buy clothes of the correct size for my beneficiaries who were far away. When I returned home, I realized how poor my decision making was in deciding the clothes sizes for other people. Of course, some of my presents did not fit anyone.

In 2015, after retiring from the seed company job in Moses Lake, in the United States, I made a trip to Tanzania to observe the activities of a seed company that had shown some interest in hiring me. Researchers from the company and I visited several farms where the company had some trials and had some fun learning how the seed business operated in Africa. The interaction between pea and bean seed companies and the chemical companies in Kenya and Tanzania was admirable. Although I could not eventually join the company, I am grateful I got a chance to visit some farms in Tanzania and gain some valuable insights.

Chapter 13

Postdoctoral Experience

While living in Germany doing my studies, I came to learn about the diversity immigrant visa program in the United States of America, which awarded fifty thousand immigrant visas each year to people from around the world. A person could apply for such a visa, and if lucky enough, one could get an opportunity to migrate legally to the United States to work and live there. We started applying for this visa program when we were still in Germany. You would go to a cybercafé and find many people, including Germans applying for the visa. In our seventh attempt and when we had already moved back to Kenya after my studies, my wife was successful. My wife won the Green Card lottery that allowed us (mother, father, and two boys) to immigrate legally and settle in the United States of America. Before my wife won the lottery, I helped others apply for the green card, and two won. After my wife got the winning letter for the green card, we started preparing for the process, which took one year and six months. We had to go for medical checkups by doctors appointed by the Embassy of the United States of America. We had to obtain the necessary documentation to allow us to travel.

We also had to decide when to write resignation letters in the places we worked and when to submit them. You did not want to tell everyone you planned to leave before you were confident everything would work as intended. We had to get any retirement benefits due to us, although these were heavily taxed. I was very fortunate to get at least a million shillings from the money I had saved through the retirement benefits insurance scheme through my employer. Getting the funds was very useful in the next phase of our lives because it gave us some little security, although we did not know what lay ahead. We attended the interview in July 2003.

On Tuesday the 15th day of July 2003, the Holy Spirit of our God was with us, and we woke up early at 3 AM to be at the American embassy at 4.30 AM. We found a sizable queue, which we joined and moved into the building to face the interviewers, who everyone feared for their tough questions. It came our turn, and we met the intelligent guys and produced every document they needed. We realized we had over-prepared ourselves and were very happy to find a very kind person with God's grace guiding her to let us through the hurdle. She congratulated us and told us to return on Thursday for the passports with visas. That was God again, sending His blessing to His people early in the morning! We

143

could not drive home immediately because we gave a ride to a girl we met at the embassy, and she had helped us with ten thousand shillings that we borrowed from her to pay for a shortfall in the visa payment. We went with her to the bank and got her the money, and we also had to help her find her uncle's home in some estate in the city.

After getting the visa in our passports, we sent our resignation letters to our employers. We also started getting our retirement benefits, cooperative contributions, and savings in our names. The money we gathered from all our funding sources was a little, but it was essential to have it in readiness for our planned move. At this juncture, we were sure we were going. We sold our belongings, selling the valuable items we could not carry. Among other items, we had a car, fridge, Television, washing machine, video camera, music player with radios, curtains, dining table, etc. A friend sold our car for us at the car bazaar in Nairobi at a reasonable price of one hundred and fifty thousand shillings just in time. We looked for an affordable one-way ticket for immigrants usually made available by the International Organization for Migration (IOM), part of the United Nations System promoting humane and orderly migration for people worldwide. We got and paid for the ticket.

The reasonably priced one-way ticket was great because it was a saving, considering we were a family of four individuals. We got a British Airways flight, which was to fly from Nairobi, Kenya, through Heathrow Airport in the United Kingdom to Seattle in the United States. From here, we were to connect with a small plane to Pullman City in Washington State in the United States of America.

Just days before the flight day, we organized farewell parties in Gatundu and Ruiru, where we bid family and friends farewell. On October third, 2003, family members and friends escorted us to the airport in an entourage of four cars and a Nissan minivan full of family and friends. In the United States, we were invited and hosted by a Nigerian host family, a great family we had the honor of meeting and living with while we lived in Germany. The host family lived in Moscow, a city in Idaho just eight miles from Pullman. The family hosted us in their house until we could get our accommodation in about two months. Our host family was composed of well-organized people who knew how to care for friends. They had prepared their house so well in advance to accommodate us. We felt very much at home, and their reception was like we were some royal family.

We immensely enjoyed and learned a few things about this family, many cultural ideas from Nigeria, and most of all, about Nigerian foods. They lived humbly and had great hearts that could accommodate all with untold warmth. They would cook very spicy Nigerian meals that were quite tasty and different from what we were used to. The delicious meals offered made life delightful, and we enjoyed learning the names of the new foods. They showed us what schools to enroll our children in and advised us when. They guided us on where to find jobs and even started introducing us to places where they worked. They were resourceful in showing

145

us how to behave in our new environment, where everything seemed different.

Learning to cope with a new environment was necessary because some people in the state of Idaho discriminate against people in racial terms. This further information meant that black people had to be careful in their social lives and watch their actions wherever they were. They showed us which supermarkets and stores sold which commodities and where you got inexpensive items. They introduced us to new friends, and our circle of friends grew, especially with friends of African origin. They helped us to navigate around and know what was where. They showed us how to open bank accounts in Moscow, Idaho, and live as respectable people. Two Kenyan and one Ugandan families with extremely loving and generous hearts were also at hand to support us in settling down. They took it upon themselves to drive us around and take us to the necessary offices. They supported us and guided us like they had always been our friends. We got jobs immediately after arrival and were fortunate enough to quickly settle down through the stable guidance of our host family. We came determined to make ends meet regardless of how difficult that task was. We were ready to do any work we got within our areas of qualifications. My wife was a Nurse, and I was a plant breeder. We arrived in Seattle on the third day of October 2003, excited about our newfound land.

The massive city of Seattle was an incredible scenery for us to behold. We saw the city from the air, were amazed at the size, and could not wait to land to see what was down there. We were delayed at the airport that day as they checked our baggage, and the small plane to Pullman left us behind. They said we could get hotel accommodation for the night and travel the following day. Yes, we looked for a hotel and found one just near the airport. We had dinner at KFC, a famous American fast-food restaurant chain. We had learned of it earlier in our stay in Germany and were excited to let our kids enjoy a treat. We got one of those family menus with many tasty chicken pieces accompanied by mashed potatoes, gravy, coleslaw, and biscuits. Everything we ate was delicious, and we slept like kings! The following morning, we were at the airport to take the small plane that took us to Pullman, Washington, where our friends were waiting to receive us. The aircraft was very uncomfortable on the way, and the children were happy when we arrived.

The host family was at the airport to welcome us and take us home to Moscow, Idaho, where they lived. Here was our first impression of rural America. It was hard to imagine because one always had a different preconceived opinion that constantly gets challenged. On Sunday, only two days after arrival, our host family introduced us to the St Augustine Catholic Church, and we went there for mass. After the mass, we retreated to a room where the people were sharing a cup of coffee and Donuts. They were warm-hearted people who welcomed us and made us feel at home. As we talked, one lady asked me what I did for work in

Kenya. I told her I was in agriculture and plant breeding. She took us to a nicely dressed man, introduced us to him, and told him I would be happy to get something to do. The newly introduced man, who turned out to be a retired professor and president at the University of Idaho, asked me when I would be ready for him to take me to Pullman and introduce me to a friend of his who was a breeder.

We made arrangements to meet on Tuesday the following week. He took me in his car to Washington State University, where we met his other friend, who told me to meet him the next Thursday to introduce me to a Pathologist who needed someone to do some work for him. I did so, and that way, I got a post-doctoral position at Washington State University starting the following Monday. I became an Associate in Research in the Plant Pathology department of Washington State University working in collaboration with the grain-legume pathologist at the USDA-ARS Research unit. The research unit was the Grain Legume Genetics and Physiology. The unit was involved in breeding and pathology research in garden peas, chickpeas, and lentils. My duties included research on the control methods of White Mold (Sclerotinia sclerotium) (biological, chemical, etc.), identifying and isolating gene(s) responsible for its determining pathogenicity on Peas, Lentils, and Chickpeas, Vegetative compatibility among sclerotinia isolates and characterization of Sclerotinia isolates and managing and development of lentil recombinant inbred lines for determining the genetics of resistance and for mapping and tagging the resistance genes. White mold is a fungal disease affecting many plants, including beans, peas, cabbage, etc. Mold symptoms are found on blossoms, stems, leaves, and pods with water-soaked spots. Leaves will wilt, yellow, and die; pods may rot. My main tasks were to investigate the chemical control of the pathogen and find an efficient way to grow spores that infect plants in white mold experiments instead of using sclerotia, which are compact masses of hardened fungal mycelium-containing food reserves. In the lab, white mold is grown on a suitable media using Sclerotia. We needed to obtain spores for infecting experimental plants in an accountable manner.

We lived in a student housing unit along Merman Drive, and we loved the location because it was close to the grocery stores, workplace, and school for the kids. I would walk to work. The kids would go to school by a school bus, and my wife was the only person working far from home, although this was just eight miles away. At first, moving around was difficult because we had no family car. Our friends from Kenya were next-door neighbors, and they would help my wife travel to Moscow, Idaho, in the morning, and she would return home by bus. Later on, I passed my driving test, and we bought our first car. Then I would give her a ride to work and go back for her in the evening. Other friends from our church would also help us with rides. We started to feel at home, and our third son was born in August 2004. He was the first person in my family to become an American citizen. The blessing of a third child became another great reason to thank God for the many graces He had bestowed upon us. His coming was a symbol of more extraordinary presents coming our way. The blessing of a child was great news because we saw some hope of becoming citizens shortly. The older boys were very helpful in taking care of the young child.

My wife worked only at night, and my bigger boys and I would stay home with the baby at night. My wife would come in the morning and stay with the baby all day. As I went to get their mother from work early in the morning, one older boy would wake up and be in charge of the baby in my absence. In the evening, the other boy would take the responsibility as I went to take their mother to work. They both learned songs to sing for the baby to calm him down. The two boys were very smart in school and it was a great joy for us to be the proud parents of extremely talented and great students. They did a lot of chores at home without complaining. One song was sung for the baby, and it just called his name, said he was good, and kept repeating it until he was calm. "Ka…. ara…nja…...ni…. mwe… ega" "Ka….ara..nja…...ni….mwe…ega". The bigger boys kept on doing well in school, attaining excellent grades. The schools in Pullman were among the best schools in Washington state.

I worked at the USDA research unit from 13 December 2003 to April 2005. A guarantee for project funding did not exist, and my boss kept asking me to look for a real job. It was hard to get another job then, but I kept trying. At this time, I could not be employed by the USDA research unit because I was not yet a citizen of the United States, and there were no vacant positions. During my time, the unit hired a new post-doctoral fellow, and he was already salivating for some of the duties of my position. I started planning to move out of the unit to go and look for something more permanent. My family and I decided to move to a bigger city with more opportunities. My wife and I resigned and served the mandatory two-week notice period.

Chapter 14

Working in the United States

In April 2005, I moved my family to Seattle, where we signed a one-year rental house lease. We registered our boys in school and started looking for jobs. I was determined to do any job to take care of my family. I got a temporary manual job where I would sign up for any job that came to the agency. I did a few such jobs that involved working for different companies around where we lived, and in most cases, the nature of the job depended on the employer. Some of the jobs involved moving stuff in boxes. One job was in a wine-making company.

During this time, I received a call from a seed company based in Moses Lake offering me an assistant plant breeder position. In Moses Lake, my family was received by a Kenyan family from Busia. With this family, we shared many experiences that shaped our lives positively. The offer came following an interview that I had done a year before.

I joined the seed company in June 2005. I would replace the incumbent breeder in two years. I aimed to apply my knowledge in plant breeding, plant pathology, and biometry to develop better varieties of green peas and beans with better yields and enhanced resistance to diseases. I wanted to serve and dedicate myself to this great opportunity. I hoped to do tremendously well and finally enjoy my career goals.

During my first ten years at the company, I was blessed with energy and wisdom by the Lord Jesus. I used my assistants' and my young kids' power and knowledge to help build a pea and bean breeding program with many more varieties released than my predecessor. My two boys worked with me in the summer for about four years. For them, this was a great way of staying out of trouble and a way for them to earn some money and gather valuable knowledge. One became an expert in selecting the most outstanding plants in the pea and bean nurseries planted in the fields. The company's owner approved him as my assistant in making plant selections after he improved in getting the desired plants with the most outstanding performance. Some days, he would wake up early and even carry a light to see plants in the morning. I worked with my predecessor for almost two years before he retired.

I used this time to learn all the essential aspects of the job from him. He was a qualified researcher who had done plant breeding for most of his life. He had gathered lots of experience working with different crops and companies. In the fall and winter, I would wake up very early, about 4.00

am, go to the greenhouse at about 5.00 am, and make crosses when everybody else was asleep. In the spring, I would work extra hard to prepare seeds for planting, then plant all generations of the breeding lines in the breeding program. In the summer, it was time to evaluate all the lines in the program. The company engaged high school kids to assist me in recording data, weeding, and harvesting the selected lines because the help from my assistants was not enough.

The program grew in productivity, and soon, I dealt with over one hundred thousand plots every year. Success in the program resulted in the development of great varieties that made the company owners consider me for great bonuses every year for several years until I retired. These bonuses were so generous they made others, especially two senior managers in the company, very jealous, so they started to find ways to frustrate my efforts so that I would find it intolerable to run for my life finally. I realized that I could never feel like a human being in this country because of the existing racial bias that polarizes all interracial interactions. I had struggled for about ten years to work very hard as the principal plant breeder at the company to contribute to science, build myself, and fend for my family. Racism was a fact of life all my years on this job. Most racist incidents were by junior staff, but the most hurting ones were by the senior people who did not find it comfortable to work with a black person. As long as a person performs their duties as they should, no one should ever use their skin color against them. In conferences, it was always difficult to feel at ease, mainly due to the mostly white crowd looking at you with disbelief. Not many black people would be at the conferences.

I used the bonus I got every year to do something for the family. The bonuses amounted to over one hundred thousand dollars annually between 2012 and 2015. In 2011, we bought three plots in Ruiru, Kenya, when my wife went to Kenya and found the plots to be worth investing in. The following year, we had a plan and built a team to build a rental building on two plots. This first team started very well and made considerable progress, especially when doing the required paperwork. The paperwork was immense, with many county officials waiting to have their hands greased before signing papers to authorize the construction. The first team also bought all the required starting materials for the foundation and did a lot of digging to remove clay soil from the ground until they hit the underlying ground rock to create the foundation.

The team built all the support pillars and the walls for the ground floor before doing a modern concrete slab. The ground floor accommodated five (5) two-bedroom and two (2) single-bedroom apartments. The first team was later replaced by a second team that continued to build, following a similar pattern and going up to the fifth floor in the next three years. New tenants would live in the new one or two-bedroom apartments whenever the contractors completed a floor. Each floor had seven flats, and we felt great about this accomplishment. It was the first time we built and finished something from the ground up. We had finally gotten a fantastic team led by members of a trust-worthy family that did all the building work supervision with the help of a devoted contractor. This construction was complete, and we could not have had a better team do this. By 2014, the building was bringing in cash, and we had attendants working for us to collect receipts from the renters once they paid their rent to the bank.

My immediate younger brother was the site caretaker as the building was being built and even after its completion. We named the rental building "Minjicare Apartments," a name that had two crucial things in it. "Minji" means Peas, and "Care" means Healthcare. My wife worked in Health care, and I worked with peas. The name, therefore, represented the contribution of both my work and my wife's work. It was another blessing that the good Lord brought our way! We had also drilled a well near the building on our other neighboring plot, and this well became the source of clean water for our tenants. The area has always had a water shortage, and this part of the city had no city water. The water was perfect for drinking and domestic use. We even tried to purify water from the well, package it in bottles, and sell it to retailers in nearby areas. This project did not succeed due to a few challenges.

Around the eighth year of my ten years working at the pea and bean breeding company, matters worsened. Before this, everything was going very well, and many successful projects led to the release of some outstanding varieties that made the company register even greater glory in the indus-try. Then came a new manager with a mission to destroy the good and replace it with the untried. He started to change the company's management, pretending that he was improving matters. He worked hand in hand with the logistics manager, who also saw me as a threat to her position in the company. In my department, they would bring in new changes in the methods of operations and new staff without consulting with me.

The new staff did not have the required education, and the manager would call them titles like "Plant breeder" to make them mock my title and make me feel belittled. The manager would also bring back those workers I had previously fired due to disrespect and the use of racial undertones and slurs. This insubordination would meet my most serious backlash. These people would feel misused and develop cold feet. They would later realize that the manager misused them, thinking he controlled everything, and they would eventually resign. These two managers thought they needed to get rid of me because I seemed to enjoy just too many privileges as a black man. So much seemed to be coming my way. In my position, I was earning the highest salary in the company due to a high bonus at the year's end. I also received the highest admiration from the company owner due to the many varieties that continued to come from the program yearly.

Pressure and insubordination eventually made me feel unworthy and uncomfortable. I started to feel demoralized, and nothing seemed to be going right. Then, my father-in-law passed away in 2014 in Kenya, and this was in June in the middle of our busy season. I had to accompany my wife for my father-in-law's last rites because we thought moral support was necessary. So, we decided to fly out for two weeks to take care of this. I made the adjustments needed and handed my work over to my assistant to take care of the department affairs in my absence. This decision to travel to Kenya made the company owner very mad, even though I was away only for two weeks and had delegated my duties appropriately. The company owner gave me a lecture like never before and told the manager about his dissatisfaction with my visit to Kenya in the previous two weeks. The communication may have triggered the increased zeal of the manager to work to my downfall. The manager would make unilateral decisions without giving me any information and even bring visitors to our breeding fields and take them around without knowing what he was showing to avoid meeting me. So, I would always see him, but he would use the other exit to avoid me. I felt that the Cold War was uncalled for. It would have been better if the manager came out and told me I was no longer serving a good purpose in the company. Work started to feel burdensome, and the idea of me resigning grew even more. It began to look like leaving was the only way to end my misery.

My life turned out to be one that had several upheavals at the Company because it became tough to please my bosses, who were unfamiliar with my role. First, it was my skin color that put someone off! Come inside and find out that the black man earns the highest in bonuses at the end of the year! Many tried to make my life feel like I was constantly under surveillance due to the terrible mistrust that arose from my being black. Being black in America makes the life of a black person difficult because most of the white people you interact with at work, as well as scientific forums, assume you know nothing even when you are more educated than them. I came to this conclusion based on the racist behavior of a couple of people who held senior positions at the company. At first, the company owner wanted to abuse the integrity of the plant breeding profession by using one young girl, an ordinary crew member who was a student who had dropped out of college.

He gave her an hourly job at first as part of my crew for two seasons, and because she was a great crew member who could drive a tractor, he uplifted her in the third season to the position of a bean breeder. Even though she had no breeding education or experience, the owner thought it was prudent because "if a black person can do it, then it can be done by anyone." This lack of professional ethics was in bad taste, and I later advised the owner to take the young person to a college first to learn basic plant breeding principles before she could work as a breeder. Of course, he did not want to do this because it would cost the company funds for college fees, and the young girl resigned. This whole season, when this young person worked as a "bean breeder," she was under so much pressure because the then crew lead and the most efficient tractor driver and crew supervisor had been transferred (after he used racist remarks) to the warehouse. A new crew lead joined the company. The new crew lead and the young girl worked together for this season. There were instances when I would give her some breeding duties, and she could not perform them because she did not accept me as an authentic authority. She would then seek advice from others not in the program, especially from the previously fired crew lead and the logistics officer. Such unruly behavior made the working situation so tense that I started being viewed as the problem because all the members of the white race would gang up and give my assistants mixed feelings about taking instructions from a black guy. The owner never made the situation any better because he would also go with the side that was not favorable to the work we were performing. This issue ended up alienating me more from the other workers.

The owner, the new manager, and the logistics officer worked together to exert pressure on me to force me out. They pushed me out of this company through racist insubordination in August 2015. I was ready to walk away with my self-respect and dignity. Humiliation would have been my next medicine. They brought the previously transferred crew lead back to the research department even when they knew we could not work together. When the owner and I first moved the previous crew lead to the warehouse, it was because he had been abusive and disrespectful to me for four straight years. As soon as he joined the company, the new Manager came up with an abrasive style of management, which saw him start changing the mode of operation even when he could not understand the basic principles. He undermined my work by sending separate divisive instructions to the research crew.

After leaving the company, the owner and his advisers proposed the new terms that would be in operation if I rejoined the company. They offered to reduce my salary by less than half if I were to go back to work for the company. In addition to this, they wanted to establish a committee to review my performance and proposed to include the same people who wanted me out of the company as the ones to determine my future fate. Both people had shown me through very clearly defined actions that they did not want me to stay by interfering continuously with chaos in the organization of the breeding program I headed. When I refused to take this abuse, they quickly hired an intern to take my place because the intern would not mind any salary offered. Their grand plan was to spoil all my chances to get a job.

They knew what to do to ruin my career for good. Several prospective employers had called the company to inquire about me. The owner of one of those employers had called me in early September and said he did not need to see my resume because he knew how much good work I had done for my previous employer. The two owners met during the December 2015 Seed Association meetings, and my last boss lied to the other owner that I had disagreed with him and convinced him how useless I was so that he could not even follow up with me to offer me the job he had promised. When I tried to follow up with the company, the owner did not want to talk to me, so I dropped my interest in pursuing this employer.

Chapter 15
Life After Formal Employment

Leaving the seed company opened my eyes. I served this company for ten years, which should have counted for something. I knew I had saved some money in the retirement plan, amounting to over three hundred thousand dollars. I started to think that investing this money would help make mortgage payments and pay university loans for our kids. The idea would be to invest this money in share and capital markets to obtain a return on investment. This idea kept motivating me to quit working in a place where I was frustrated and unhappy and had even started to have unexplained headaches.

The headaches continued until I gathered enough courage to let my family know my thought process concerning retirement, and they all agreed that it was just about the right time to turn to another page. The last day of work was the 31st of August 2015, and I was relieved that the day had finally dawned. This great day would mark the beginning of my retirement life. This day was a blessed one because it marked the first day of freedom from from formal employment. It was the day when I realized that I could make my own timetable and carry out my own plans without anyone checking on my performance. Although retirement life was still unbeknown to me, I was looking forward to long-lasting rest, freedom in time management, resource management, being with family, traveling, and all other benefits of retirement. I was not sure what was coming and was anxious about the future. I looked for a plant breeding job in my state and the surrounding states.

Getting a job was just a hope that never came to be. My employer blocked all my chances to advance. The owner lied to all prospective employers that I had signed a non-compete agreement that denied me getting a job in the industry. The manager who made me leave the company also lied to another prospective employer. That meant that no jobs would be available for me in the area around home. I then focused on finding employment in the region but started to give up hope. Still, whenever a prospective employer called for information about me, the former employer would lie, making the prospective employer quit looking for me. The prospective employer would ignore my application. In the meantime, I took the retirement plan money and invested all of it in a stock market company. The funds remained invested in the investment company for about one year.

We did not earn that much because the year saw a lot of instability in the stock market, and we thought it wise to get it back and invest it in real estate where we thought there were more earnings. We had waited for too long without any major improvements in the market situation. Very minor changes occurred in the stock market, and the investment seemed terrible. We were interested in buying old houses and remodeling them for resale. We remodeled two houses and gathered substantial experience working with different contractors. An outstanding real estate agent helped us with house acquisition, remodeling ideas, and selling the homes. The real estate agent was also a valuable resource for getting contractors and getting loans for the work. Although we only made a little money from flipping the two houses, we gathered some practical experience as we learned new techniques and procedures for making money. We also learned a lot about the housing market.

I was in Kenya between December 2015 and April 2016, trying to set up a pure water supply company. The beverage company was registered as Sifa and located in Ruiru town in our Mijicare building. The water business had management and technical problems for about three years and had to be closed down. From March 2016, I kept myself busy doing routine home maintenance chores, including mowing the lawns, feeding our goats, and managing our gardens. I was also involved in day-to-day bookkeeping and record keeping for our Blue Goose Care Center business. Our business is an adult family home business where my wife manages caregivers to provide personal care for up to six elderly clients per home. My other role in the business was handling the monthly billing and bank reconciliation needed to keep the business afloat. In 2017, we acquired a mortgage to operate a rental building with four apartments, which we got by putting down two hundred thousand dollars from my retirement package. Acquisition of this rental was a significant step because we started earning a little income without going to work. It is a good project because some money comes every month without having to do anything except to pay the mortgage.

The difference between the gross income and expenditure left a two thousand-plus profit. In the same year, we acquired a lot to construct a second adult-family home. I started working on the lot by clearing the natural vegetation by running up and down with a tractor. The plot was 1.28 acres and was fairly flat, although it also had a reasonable slope. The natural vegetation was mainly shrubs like sagebrush and bitterbrush, as well as native forbs and grasses. These were relatively easy to work with. The next step was to make a fence around the plot. We decided we wanted a six-foot-high fence made of chain link.

I looked up the information on how to do this from the YouTube channel and consulted a distributor of fencing materials who helped me get all the needed materials. I installed the fence with the complete set of materials, but it took me several months to fence the whole perimeter completely. When necessary, my friend from Busia, who was always ready to work with me on several projects, helped me pull the fence to make it tight and secure. The holes needed for the posts required to be two feet deep. One of the reasons the fence installation took longer was the presence of rocks in the ground. The best part was the concrete job, where you would preset the post using levels and ropes and then pour a dry concrete mixture before mixing it with water to wet it. You would then use a stake to properly mix the water and the concrete from the bottom to the top of the hole. The gates were also specially designed per my specifications and delivered for me to install them. I did this as recommended by the fence company. It felt great to complete the fence task in the middle of 2018. My wife and I planted 180 trees next to the fence along its perimeter. It was hard work because we decided to make a large trench instead of digging holes for the trees.

Another significant development was the construction of a concrete four-foot-wide walkway about three hundred feet long in the backyard. We constructed the walkway as a therapeutic walkway where a resident in a wheelchair can be wheeled around the backyard to enjoy the sunshine, especially in the summer. I did the walkway's initial site preparation, which involved ground leveling, laying gravel, compacting the gravel, and tying and laying rebars. My son Peter was my assistant in this project. The next step was to pour the concrete and finish it. We hired a professional team to do the last step. The professional team came on the last day and did a tremendous finishing job. The construction of the house started in the fall of 2017 and concluded in September of 2018. A local mortgage company provided the construction loan.

The contractor was a small construction company we had previously contracted to add an extra room in our first business house. This contractor gave his estimate to the mortgage company, which approved the construction loan. The house construction occurred step-by-step, clearing the building costs systematically. The agreement was that the general contractor would look for sub-contractors who gave bids stating how much they would charge to do a particular task, starting from the site preparation to the foundation, footings, crawlspace, garage and slab, framing, exterior masonry, sheathing for external windows, doors, walls, HVAC system, plumbing, installation of electrical wires, roofing, insulation, drywall and so on. The builders closely followed the process. Immediately after a task was completed, the contractor would inspect the work and call the mortgage company, which would send an inspector. We would sign the invoice, and it would go to the mortgage company to process the payment. Then, we would move to the next task until the whole house was ready. The building experience was such a great experience for me because the process differed from what I had experienced in Kenya.

The house was about five thousand square feet and had eight bedrooms. The vast space was necessary because it had private rooms with bathrooms to accommodate six clients, a family area with two bedrooms, and a nine hundred square feet family room. We designed and had a Gazebo built behind the house for residents to shelter in whenever they came outside the house. I measured about a hundred feet from the road to decide the house's location on the lot. It was necessary to reduce the noise from cars on the road. It was also necessary to keep future residents safe if they wander off to the road. Also, if residents make unnecessary noise, it would not disturb passers-by. One other exciting development was designing the driveway and setting up irrigation sprinklers.

The U-shaped driveway allowed vehicles to pull in and out without reversing. This kind of driveway also allows ample spacing in the front yard. I learned how to set up irrigation sprinkler systems, dig trenches, lay down the pipes, and install the sprinklers. I set up a soccer goal and net for my sons to play soccer whenever they come home. By January 2019, this house started operations as our second adult family home. In Washington State, an adult family home is a residential home licensed to care for two to six adults not related by blood or marriage to the person or persons providing the services. The home offers room and meals, laundry, supervision, assistance with activities of daily living, and personal care. My wife was the manager responsible for supervising our establishment's residents' care and caregivers. The new house increased my work in estate management, office management and bookkeeping tasks. We also acquired a bus with a wheelchair lift to transport residents in wheelchairs to doctor appointments and shopping. The bus acquisition created a new responsibility for me as a bus driver.

In the fall of 2021, we acquired another mortgage to purchase a third adult-family home. We got the residence after a thorough search of single-family residences in the area that were big enough and sold at a reasonable price. The other consideration was to get a lender capable of giving us a mortgage fitting our needs. Getting the home was tough. First, all the lenders we had used before had one or two reasons for rejecting to offer the mortgage for this project, although the reasons were beyond the co-borrower's control. Secondly, the main house had a smaller three-bedroom mobile home on its side, and some lenders refused to fund such a project. We finally got an agreeable lender with funds to support the project.

The county required us to obtain a conditional land use permit that required the collection of comments from the neighbors as to whether or not they supported the idea of our home becoming an adult family home. The county requested comments from neighbors living within a three-hundred feet radius. They also wanted comments from city or county officials who would testify if any factor would prevent the house from being licensed to operate. A judge would hear the comments and later decide whether or not to issue the permit. The county approved the permit at the end of the process, and we were ready to go to the next step. We remodeled the home by widening doors, making them wheelchair accessible, installing grab bars, installing a gate, creating a bigger washroom, installing a ramp, installing concrete around the building to enhance cleanliness, and building a porch at the back. We engaged different contractors for the various jobs but faced many difficulties and delays due to COVID-19, an epidemic that year. After we completed the main jobs, we sent an application for a license to the Licensor. This process took a lot of time, from April to October, when we got a reply. By the end of December 2022, we got the license and decided to start operating in January 2023.

Chapter 16
Conclusion

My life journey is a blessed one. A series of significant happenings in my life indicated some blessings. These happenings included my closing high school examinations when I had the best performance in our school's national examinations; when I had the highest performance in company law in accounting; I was the first one in my family ever to join a university; I had the best performance in plant breeding at the University of Nairobi Master of science program; when I had the best performance in an international pre-Masters of Science examination in plant breeding in holland and many other firsts. The journey had very many turns that took me to different colleges and countries where I got different experiences. The adventures also affected my wife and children similarly or in other ways. The experiences must have blessed my family significantly and molded my children into great citizens. The many blessings came in large numbers and surrounded me, so I was selected out of many others on many occasions. It meant that the good Lord had spared me some special graces. The beginning of all my graces was being born by God-fearing parents who brought me up with my eight siblings. On the way, I made numerous friends who filled my life with untold joy and immensely contributed to making the journey more enjoyable. This joy in my life became the common thread that joined all events, making it worth celebrating and giving me many reasons to thank my creator, who was responsible for every part of it.

The most important of all my blessings are perhaps those of my lifelong partner and wife of many years, Veronica Wanjiku Nganga, and my three children, James Wamatu, Stephen Wabeti, and Peter Karanja. This gift of family made me the kind of person I am today. The family means a lot to me, and this is what moves my life forward. From the day I met my wife, she always added great stuff to my life. It is from the deep love from her heart to filling my pots, plates, and cups to the brim. This great lady continuously fills my life with effort, energy, materials, spiritual support, and so many different goodies that she finds. It is like she finds and collects different stuff to bring home for us to enjoy ourselves. She has been a fantastic helper for our children and extended families and me. She took "this man to have and to hold from this day forward for better and for worse 'till death do us part." She said these words before God on December 21, 2001, and sincerely kept her word.

We have always shared what we have, whether good or bad. We keep consoling one another in bad moments and celebrate great moments together. We have learned to enjoy life together without complaint. We have also learned to be grateful for anything we receive from the Almighty God. The journey feels easier, lighter, and shorter when discussing incoming events. Veronica endured great difficulties when she arrived at our home as she tried to fit in. She overcame the attitude of some of the people and came out victorious, becoming a winner of many hearts. When she joined my family, Veronica worked hard to become an important extended family member. She planted many crops, including bananas, corn, beans, arrow roots, Napier grass for cows, and many others. She worked tirelessly to avoid naysayers who always moved around in the village, calling others lazy. She would end up extremely tired at the end of the day. She also looked after our cow and was very good at milking. She courageously deals with my alter ego and tries to tame and steer me forward positively. We have always shared our journey and appreciated the roles played by our children in keeping the family on its toes.

Veronica, our home nurse, is in charge of all medical matters. She takes care of all our medical needs. No questions asked! She makes my life easy to endure, even at the time when I had sugar issues and needed insulin injections, she was always there to monitor everything from the medicines to the food that we took. She is our chef too! Any dish you can imagine and order becomes available when you ask her to make it. She made sure all meals were warm and had drinks to go with. Sometimes, I wondered what kind of magic she possessed in cooking! A meal that would take me an hour to make would only take her a few minutes. The meal would be well presented and would taste marvelous. She has always been excellent in our investment division at home. She remains a great adviser on our development agenda and has spearheaded most of our investment drives. She is also great at making important home decisions. She is vital in deciding the clothes to wear for which occasion, what color of curtain makes more sense, which shoes fit you best, what food to cook, who gets the invitation, what to do, etc. You can, therefore, not ignore her if you want a sound decision.

I know this from experience. We have helped many people in various ways, including medical and financial. Veronica is great at following medical orders, and her whole life is full of caring moments. Older adults are the primary beneficiaries. Her current occupation involves caring for older adults in our adult family homes. She cares for them with the highest level of compassion and deep commitment. She has made many friends this way, and people always come back to thank her. The children were very active as our cheerleaders, thereby making our journey busy and worthwhile with no time to waste. Their encouragement was palpable but necessary. They volunteered to help me with the memoir when they learned of it. Their moral support was considerable with the constant words of advice. They helped me learn many new things, especially those related to new technologies, and they also did great in being comrades in a journey where all were active participants in the many experiences we gained. They did multiple tasks in their lives to make our lives better. Their mother and I gave them many chores that they completed well and to our total satisfaction.

About the Author

John Nganga Wamatu wrote this memoir as an account of the blessed experiences in his life. He holds a Ph.D. in Agricultural Science from the Humboldt University in Berlin, Germany, a Master of Science in Plant Breeding, and a Bachelor of Science in agriculture degrees from the University of Nairobi, Kenya. He is a plant breeder who worked for fifteen years at the Coffee Research Foundation in Kenya and ten years as a pea and bean breeder at a seed company in the USA. John developed many outstanding pea and bean varieties. He lives in Moses Lake, Washington, with his wife and family. He and his wife co-founded the Blue Goose Care Centers adult family homes.

www.ingramcontent.com/pod-product-compliance
Lightning Source LLC
Chambersburg PA
CBHW052045090426
42739CB00010B/2053